Cooking in a Small Kitchen

Cooking in a Small Kitchen

By Arthur Schwartz
Illustrated by Gary Rogers

LITTLE, BROWN AND COMPANY   Boston – Toronto

Library of Congress Cataloging in Publication Data

Schwartz, Arthur R
  Cooking in a small kitchen.
  Includes index.
  1. Cookery, 2. Kitchens. 3. Kitchen utensils.
I. Title.
TX 652.S39   641.5   78–27148
ISBN 0–316–77565–7

MV
Designed by Janis Capone

*Published simultaneously in Canada
by Little, Brown & Company (Canada) Limited*

PRINTED IN THE UNITED STATES OF AMERICA

For Brian,
who will find at least a few of the family treasures here.

Contents

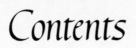

Cooking in a Small Kitchen

Introduction

The largest kitchen I have ever worked in was a luxurious twenty feet long by twelve feet wide and equipped with every conceivable modern convenience. I hated it.

It was beautiful to look at and had acres of counter space. But by the end of a day of cooking I had walked so many miles from the stove to the refrigerator, from the refrigerator to the vegetable cleaning sink, from the sink to the "baking center," from the "baking center" to the chopping block, and from the chopping block back to the stove, that my feet were numb with pain.

I suppose as a reaction to this inconveniently large room, I decided that in the next kitchen I had, a more modest ten-by-ten affair open to a dining area, I would hone down my work space to a neat little square with the refrigerator behind me, the stove in front of me, the sink and a short length of counter to the left, and a chopping area to the right. I wasn't using the whole room, but it fulfilled rather demanding needs and I never had to move from one spot.

This seems to me the best of all possible kitchen arrangements and, as a city dweller, probably the one and only perfect kitchen I will ever be lucky enough to have. The city kitchens I am familiar with, even those that are adequately equipped, are cramped at best. You have to balance the chopping board on the edge of the sink, and too bad if you have to rinse a plate. There's no place to set down a fork, much less a pot lid. And if you aren't careful, you could step in the garbage while just turning around.

When the city kitchen is bad, it is really bad. The landlords call them kitchenettes. You laugh at the pretension and eat out a lot — secure in the excuse that your kitchen is too small to cook in — and you never invite anyone to dinner.

There are, to be sure, more than a few logistical problems when cooking in a kitchen the size of a closet. But you'd be surprised how organization, common sense, and a desire to eat well can conspire to produce a delicious, even sophisticated, meal. The small size of your kitchen actually dictates a few of the basic rules of good, basic cooking and sensible eating. You'll have to start each recipe well organized. You must rely mostly on fresh ingredients because you haven't much room to store food. Your dishes must be fairly simple because there's no storage space for a lot of pots, pans, serving pieces, or tableware. Often you'll have to cook in one pot. And, you have to concentrate on three-course menus because you can't cook too many dishes at once on your small range.

I hope in this book to show how you can eat well from food cooked in your closet kitchen — how to manage with only two burners, how to eliminate steps that require counter space you don't have, how to organize recipes for ahead-of-time preparation, and how to plan menus geared to your tiny workroom. I hope, as well, that you'll be able to learn some basics of cooking and eating that will see you through more palatial kitchens.

And when times get really rough in your little closet, when you've knocked one too many precariously placed pots onto the floor and your last wineglass has just cracked from the weight of the pasta-filled colander you put on it, just remember, at least your feet don't hurt.

Equipment and Logistics

With food processors, microwave ovens, electric slow-cookers, Crock Pots, mini-fryers, hamburger grills, and almost restaurant-sized mixers permeating the market, it's become amazing to some people that excellent food can be produced with rather simple, even primitive, equipment. A three-quart saucepan, a ten-inch skillet, a sharp knife, a large mixing bowl, and a wooden spoon supplemented by a soupspoon, a dinner fork, and a coffee cup can get you pretty far. I don't recommend it but it can be done.

To that list I would at least add:

A teakettle for boiling water
A filter drip coffeepot
An eight- or ten-inch French chef's knife
A slotted metal kitchen spoon
An enameled cast-iron or earthenware casserole that can be used on top of of the stove and in the oven and is attractive enough to go to the table
An eight-inch skillet for cooking eggs, among other things
A deep twelve-inch, straight-sided heavy aluminum sauté pan with cover for cooking chicken, stews, and Chinese stir-fry dishes
An eight-quart enameled cast iron casserole for boiling pasta, making stews, pot roasts, and large quantities of soup

It also would be helpful to have:

Another wooden spoon
A rubber spatula
A large strainer for draining pasta and other foods and also for pureeing some foods
One-cup and four-cup heatproof glass measuring cups
Metal measuring spoons on a ring
An attractive ceramic pie plate to double as a baking dish that can go to the table
A four-sided stainless steel grater

A stainless steel wire whisk
A stainless steel swivel-bladed vegetable peeler
A baking sheet, preferably a jelly roll pan that has four half-inch sides
A can opener
A small mixing bowl

In fact, with the exception of some baking pans and an inexpensive electric hand mixer, you could prepare almost all the recipes in this book with just this equipment. Certainly you can eat quite well. There are a few additional utensils, however, that I feel are necessary for a small kitchen or are simply valuable tools beyond this basic kitchen battery.

Two touted pieces of culinary equipment are the food processor and the microwave oven. Food processors are the best thing to happen to kitchens and cooks in a long time, but I think the case for owning a microwave oven is somewhat dubious. A well-made food processor will slice, chop, puree, grate, and mix. It takes up very little counter space and can save enormous amounts of time and effort, especially if you cook often. I'm not sure it's worth the investment to someone who doesn't cook much, and I'm quite positive it is worthless unless you have the counter space to keep it handy at all times. But even if I had just a tiny amount of space to spare for it I would own a food processor. And I'd much prefer to clutter the counter with a food processor than a toaster. I toast bread in the broiler or oven.

A food processor is not an absolute requirement of any recipe in this book, but it is suggested for special jobs, such as pureeing, for which it has no peers. Until food processors became available a few years ago, almost everyone used a blender for pureeing foods. And if you have a blender you will find a number of uses for it here. If you don't own one, however, I don't recommend going out now and buying it. A food processor, although more expensive, is a better value. An old-fashioned food mill, which forces food through a sharp mesh, can also puree well and it is, of course, the least expensive pureer you can find. It also has the virtue of having a hole in the handle for hanging it out of the way of the work surface, but obviously more time and energy is required to puree with a food mill than with a food processor.

Microwave ovens seem to me to have limited uses considering their expense and the amount of space they consume. From my experience, they do not cook many foods nearly as satisfactorily as conventional methods do—roasts emerge with a steamed taste and texture, bread and cheese become rubbery even at low temperatures, large amounts of vegetables take much longer to cook, it's impossible to cook an egg with the yolk runny and the white set. What a microwave can do beautifully is soften or melt butter in seconds, fry bacon crisp between paper towels, reheat leftovers, defrost frozen foods, and reheat coffee without ruining the flavor—none of which seem to me worth its considerable cost. There also still seems to be some question about the safety of microwaves in general.

At the other end of the kitchen equipment spectrum, there is a very inexpensive kitchen gadget that I would't be without—a plastic Mouli nut and cheese grater. This is a small rotary grater that will grind nuts without their becoming pasty and grate cheese without fuss. I recommend the plastic model because, unlike the metal models with interchangeable graters, large pieces cannot leak from the plastic grater. The carriage cylinder is sealed.

The biggest problem of all in a small kitchen, however, is finding a place to chop, slice, and otherwise prepare vegetables and other foods for the pot. Assuming you have little or no counter space, the most useful piece of equipment you can probably buy is a board that will hinge over your sink. You can buy both wooden and sturdy plastic models with a strategically placed hole through which water can run into the sink. Some of these models also have strainers that fit into the hole so that you don't stop up the sink with vegetable scraps. Slicing, dicing, and other less vigorous ways of cutting up food can be done on a sink board, but heavy chopping of such things as parsley or garlic may have to be done on a sturdier surface. It's also a good idea to learn how to cut up some foods directly over the pot without cutting yourself. Cutting carrots against the thumb is an old homemaker's habit and a good one to acquire if you have no other place to cut carrots.

In older buildings, no matter how tiny the kitchen, there is often a double sink with a drainboard that fits over one half. It should not be used as a drainboard if it can be put to better advantage. In modern kitchens there is generally a single sink sunken into a counter, or at least a counter ledge, and no drainboard. In both cases, look into the possibility of hanging a plastic-coated wire or wooden dish-drain rack over the sink area. These are now widely available in housewares stores. One acquaintance of mine had her two cabinets moved up higher than usual so she could fit a drain rack under one and a combination cookbook and spice shelf under the other. She has to stand on a stool to reach the top shelves of her cupboards, but she has gained about four square feet of working space in a kitchen that has a total of about six square feet of floor space.

Portable surfaces can also be used to gain a place to put something down. By this I mean surfaces that can be worked on or over, then be disposed of or carried out of the kitchen until needed. A baking sheet or jelly roll pan, for instance, can be lined with paper towels or plain brown paper bags (when either one will do, the recipe will call for absorbent paper) to drain fried or greasy foods. And it can be used as a surface to assemble vegetables for a Chinese dish. Another portable surface is paper toweling. Never peel or clean a vegetable on your little bit of counter space. Do it on a piece of paper towel so it can be scooped away easily and without soiling the space needed for chopping. It may not be ecologically sound, but it is practical. I use many small bowls – soup bowls and cereal bowls – and plastic containers as portables. I put prepared ingredients in them and keep them out of the way in the refrigerator, on the refrigerator, on the window sill or in the next room until they are needed.

Although there may not be anything you can do about this piece of equipment, gas ranges are highly preferable to electric ones in a small kitchen. When a cooking period is over, you have to remove a pot from the coil of an electric stove to get it to stop cooking because the coil remains hot for minutes after you've turned it off. And when you have to remove a pot from the stove, there has to be someplace else to put it. With a gas range, however, when you turn the heat off, the range cools immediately and therefore the pot doesn't have to be moved. This all sounds rather obvious, so you must see the ramifications for a small kitchen. An electric range increases the necessity of juggling pots, pans, and plates, while a gas range can become another work surface. When dredging food in flour before frying or browning, for instance, I generally place the plate of flour on the gas burner next to the skillet. I'll also place a plate to receive fried or browned food on the burners not being used. If I had an electric stove I couldn't be so liberal with this range space, because every time I turned off the burner under the skillet, the burner would remain hot for quite a while.

Organization is, above all, an essential if you wish to produce more than an omelet or meat loaf. Dinner parties call for list making. Ingredients should be prepared before you start cooking. You should be well acquainted with the recipe before starting to cook. But these are all good cooking habits, whether your kitchen is small or large.

Soups

Many soup recipes are ideal for a small kitchen. All they require is one pot to boil in and one burner to cook on. The menus in this chapter start out with soups to feed smaller numbers—one, two, and four—and they can all be prepared in a three-quart saucepan or a slightly smaller one in some cases. The next group serves about six persons, and for some of these you will need a slightly larger pot. The last few recipes feed eight to twelve, and for these a large casserole is needed.

A number of the recipes here, the lighter ones, are for soups that you would serve only as a first course. But there are an equal number which you could feature as the main event followed by just a salad.

QUICK KIDNEY BEAN SOUP

A can of beans heated with a few seasonings and broth or bouillon makes a comforting soup for a quick meal taken in solitude.

*1 1-pound 4-ounce can red
  kidney beans
2 cloves garlic, crushed
1 tablespoon olive oil
1/2 teaspoon thyme*

*1 tablespoon tomato paste
1/2 cup chicken broth or bouillon
Salt and fresh-ground black pepper
  to taste*

1. Pour the beans and their liquid into a small saucepan. With a wooden spoon, mash up at least half the beans.

2. Add the remaining ingredients, stir well and simmer gently for 15 minutes. Add more broth if too thick. Adjust seasoning to taste.
Makes 1 generous serving.

COLD CRAB BISQUE

You can pack this into a thermos to begin an intimate picnic lunch of ham sandwiches on biscuits, raw vegetables with a dip, and fresh fruit. Or serve it indoors before broiled fish, the fish baked with vegetables on page 162 or a main course salad such as the noodle salad on page 55.

4 tablespoons butter
4 tablespoons flour
1 cup bottled clam juice
1 cup milk
1/2 cup heavy cream
1 teaspoon lemon juice
8 ounces crabmeat, fresh or
  thawed frozen

1/4 cup dry sherry
Pinch cayenne pepper
Salt to taste
2 hard-boiled eggs, chopped
  (optional, for garnish)

1. In a 2- to 3-quart saucepan, melt butter over medium heat. Blend in flour and cook over low heat for about 3 minutes without browning the flour. Remove from heat and allow bubbling to subside.

2. Add clam juice, milk, and cream, stirring constantly with a wooden spoon or wire whisk. Return to medium heat and, stirring constantly, bring to a boil. Lower heat and simmer gently for about 5 minutes.

3. Meanwhile, pick over the crabmeat and remove any shell or cartilage. Flake most of the crabmeat, but reserve 4 good-sized pieces for garnish.

4. Add the lemon juice, crabmeat, sherry, cayenne pepper, and salt. Heat through without boiling. Remove from heat. Chill very well before serving.

5. Check seasoning before serving and garnish each cup with large pieces of crab and chopped egg. *Makes 2 generous servings.*

OYSTER SOUP

Here you have a recipe that is so easy, yet so elegant, that you might be tempted to make it all the time if oysters weren't so pricey.

3 tablespoons butter
6 large shallots, chopped fine
1 rib celery, chopped fine
24 fresh, shucked oysters with
   the liquid from their shells

2 bay leaves
Salt and pepper to taste
2 teaspoons red-wine or sherry
   vinegar

1. In a 2- to 3-quart saucepan, melt the butter over medium-low heat and sauté shallots and celery until tender, about 10 minutes.

2. Strain the oysters from their liquid, letting the liquid drain into a 4-cup measuring cup. Add enough water to make 4 cups of liquid. Add liquid to sautéed vegetables. Add bay leaves. Season to taste with salt and pepper. Add vinegar. Bring to a boil, reduce heat and simmer gently, uncovered, for 15 to 20 minutes. (May be prepared ahead to this point.)

3. Just before serving, add the oysters to the simmering broth. Bring nearly to the boil, then serve immediately. *Makes 4 servings.*

Quick variation: A less successful version, but one that's good to know about in an emergency, can be made with canned oysters. Use two 8-ounce cans of oysters instead of the fresh ones. Drain them and add the water to the can liquid. Remove from heat as soon as you add the canned oysters to the simmering broth.

BREAD AND ANY ALLIUM SOUP

Allium is the family name for such members of the lily family as shallots, garlic, onions, and leeks. Any one of them will work in this peasanty bread-thickened cream soup. Which allium you use, as well as which dairy enrichment, depends entirely on whim and which is handy at the moment. This is obviously a good soup to know about when you're too lazy to shop. The bread thickening is called a *panade* in this soup's native France and some sources call the whole soup a panade.

6 slices firm white bread
2 cups milk
1 tablespoon butter
1 cup coarse-chopped shallots, or 10 large cloves garlic, chopped coarse, or 1-1/2 cups coarse-chopped leeks or onions

2 cups chicken broth
Salt and fresh-ground black pepper to taste
Dash nutmeg
1 cup heavy cream, sour cream, yogurt, or milk (or a combination)

1. Cut the crusts off the bread and break the dough into small pieces. Discard the crusts. In a mixing bowl, combine the milk and bread. Set aside to soak.

2. In a 2- to 3-quart saucepan, melt the butter over medium heat. Add the allium of your choice and sauté for 1 minute. Add the chicken broth and bring to a simmer over medium heat.

3. Meanwhile, mash the bread to a pulp with a wooden spoon or puree the bread and milk in a food processor or blender.

4. Add the bread paste to the saucepan and beat vigorously with a wire whip or wooden spoon. Let simmer for about 15 minutes or until bread is totally dissolved and soup has thickened.

5. Stir in the cream, yogurt, or milk. Season with salt, pepper and nutmeg. Heat through to serving temperature. If too thick, add more broth or cream. If too thin, add some breadcrumbs and heat through. Serve with a pepper mill for each diner to grind extra pepper to taste. *Makes 4 generous servings.*

PEANUT SOUP

As American as apple pie.

3 tablespoon butter
1 small onion, chopped fine
1 small rib celery, chopped fine
3 tablespoons flour
1 quart chicken broth
1 cup smooth 100% natural
  peanut butter

1 cup half-and-half (milk and
  light cream)
Salt to taste
Fresh-ground black pepper to
  taste

1. In a 3-quart saucepan, melt the butter over medium-low heat and sauté onions and celery slowly, until soft but not browned, about 15 minutes.

2. Blend in the flour and continue to cook over medium heat about 5 minutes or until flour is golden. Remove from heat and allow bubbling to subside.

3. Add the broth, stirring constantly with a wooden spoon or wire whisk. Place over high heat and, stirring constantly, bring to a boil. Lower heat and simmer gently for about a minute.

4. Stir in the peanut butter until completely dissolved. (At this point, the soup may be pureed in a food mill, blender, or food processor if you want a smoother texture, although personally I like it slightly coarse.)

5. Stir in half-and-half, season with salt and pepper, and reheat to serving temperature. Serve with garlic croutons, if desired. *Makes 4 servings.*

JULES BOND'S CONSOMMÉ WITH GARDEN VEGETABLES

Jules Bond, a food authority of international stature who lives on Shelter Island in the middle of Peconic Bay, once offered this soup as part of a menu composed entirely of Long Island foods — garden vegetables, striped bass, Muscovy ducks, and Hargrave Vineyard wines. Jules is truly one of the most food-loving people I know, but as you can see from the use of canned broth here, he is not against an occasional cooking shortcut.

3 13-3/4-ounce cans beef broth
1 pound lean ground beef
2 to 3 white (inner) ribs celery, roughly cut up
2 medium carrots, diced
2 white (inner) ribs celery, diced
1/2 yellow summer squash (or 1 very small one), diced

1/4 pound green beans, diced
1/4 pound wax beans, diced
1 medium potato, peeled and diced
2 tablespoons Madeira (Bond uses a sweet Boal type)

1. In a 3-quart saucepan, combine the broth, ground beef, and roughly cut celery. Partially cover and simmer gently for about 1-1/2 hours, skimming off scum as necessary.

2. Strain, then refrigerate until fat solidifies on top, at least several hours. Skim carefully.

3. Reheat the consommé and cook the diced carrots until tender. Remove carrots with a slotted spoon and set aside in a bowl. Cook the diced celery until tender and add it to the bowl. Cook the squash. Cook both types of beans together, remove them, then cook the potato. If necessary, add enough water to the consommé to make about 4 cups. (Soup and vegetables can be done ahead to this point.)

4. Just before serving, bring the consommé to a simmer and add the cooked vegetables and Madeira. Check the seasoning and heat through. *Makes 4 servings.*

BROCCOLI AND SHELL MACARONI SOUP

Enough for a light vegetarian supper with a cheese board, bread, and wine.

3 tablespoons olive oil
1 medium onion, chopped
1 large clove garlic, chopped
1 rib celery, chopped
2 tablespoons chopped parsley
1/2 teaspoon dried marjoram
1 1-pound can plum tomatoes
  with the juice

1/2 bunch broccoli
6 cups chicken broth, beef broth,
  or water
1 cup small macaroni shells
Salt and fresh-ground pepper to
  taste
1/2 cup fresh grated Romano
  cheese (approximately)

1. In a 3-quart saucepan, combine the olive oil, onion, garlic, celery, parsley, and marjoram. Cook over medium heat until vegetables are tender.

2. Add the tomatoes and their juice, break up the tomatoes with a wooden spoon, and simmer for 15 minutes.

3. Meanwhile, cut the top of the broccoli into small flowerets and the stems into small pieces.

4. Add the broccoli and liquid and bring to a simmer. Season to taste with salt and pepper. Simmer 5 minutes. (Can be prepared ahead to this point. Return to a simmer before continuing.)

5. Add the shells and continue to simmer until shells are tender, about 15 minutes. Correct seasoning if necessary and serve immediately. Stir in cheese or serve separately. *Makes 4 generous servings.*

CREAM OF MUSHROOM SOUP

The good dose of sherry in this recipe helps compensate for the blandness of most commercial mushrooms.

6 tablespoons butter (1 1/4 -
  pound stick)
3/4 pound mushrooms, sliced
  thin
1/3 cup dry sherry
1/4 teaspoon nutmeg

Salt and fresh-ground pepper
  to taste
6 tablespoons flour
1-3/4 cups beef broth
2 cups milk or 1 cup milk and 1
  cup heavy cream

1. In a 3-quart saucepan, melt the butter over medium heat and sauté mushrooms for about 3 minutes.

2. Add the sherry, nutmeg, salt, and pepper. Simmer gently, stirring often, until all the mushroom liquid and sherry have evaporated.

3. With a wooden spoon, blend in the flour, and continue to cook over medium heat until flour is golden, about 4 minutes. Remove from heat and let the bubbling subside.

4. Add the broth and milk, stirring constantly, then return to medium heat. Bring to a simmer, stirring constantly, then simmer, uncovered, about 15 minutes. Taste and correct seasoning, if necessary. Serve very hot. *Makes 4 servings.*

THICK RICE SOUP

This is what the Chinese would call a congee and they might eat this as a light meal in itself — not a bad idea for a quick supper or Sunday afternoon restorative. Also serve it before broiled chicken or fish or teriyaki-style chicken (see page 165).

6 cups chicken broth or bouillon
1 cup raw rice
1/4 teaspoon ground ginger
1/2 10-ounce box frozen tiny peas
1/2 10-ounce box frozen chopped spinach
Salt to taste
2 eggs
2 scallions, sliced thin (including green part)

1. In a 3-quart saucepan, bring the broth to a boil. Add the rice and ginger, cover and simmer for 30 minutes or until rice is just about disintegrated.

2. Stir in the peas, spinach, and salt and return to a boil.

3. In a small bowl or cup, beat the eggs very well, then drizzle them a little at a time into the boiling soup. Do not stir, but let the soup simmer another 5 minutes or so. Garnish each bowl with chopped scallion. *Makes 4 servings.*

A TUSCAN BEAN SOUP

This is only one of the many bean soups made in Tuscany, but one with which I have a particularly fond association. It was served in the grandeur of Piero and Lorenza Stucchi's twelfth-century monastery kitchen in Gaiola, in front of an enormous cooking hearth. In the soup we floated the traditional *crostini* — thin, dried, whole wheat bread — and the fabulous green Tuscan oil pressed from the olives that grow alongside the grapes in the Chianti vineyards.

The rest of the menu, which was at least partially prepared by Signora Stucchi, who among her other pursuits translates foreign cookbooks into Italian, consisted of *carpaccio* — thin raw strips of beef topped with slivered raw wild mushrooms, lemon juice, and olive oil (see page 67) — the best eggplant Parmesan casserole I have ever eaten — made with fresh plum tomatoes and Gruyère instead of mozzarella — and, for dessert, a rich almond cake.

The Stucchi estate, not so incidentally, produces one of the finest wines of the Chianti classico region, Badia a Coltibuono. The wine is unfortunately not available here at the moment. At this dinner in Gaiola, however, we drank plenty of it, in various vintages, including the wine of my birth year.

A fruity olive oil is all-important in this recipe, as it is for most Tuscan cooking, but you won't be able to buy the best Tuscan oil. Try instead to use the more readily available virgin oil from Spain rather than the overrefined olive oil imported from Lucca. The Lucca oil available in supermarkets may be legitimately Tuscan, but it's nothing like the real farm product.

1 pound dried white kidney (cannellini) beans	1 cup chicken or meat broth
1 quart cold water	1/4 teaspoon sweet marjoram
1/4 cup olive oil	Salt and fresh-ground black pepper to taste
1 medium onion, chopped fine	1 bunch beet greens, washed and chopped or 1/2 10-ounce package frozen chopped spinach
1 small carrot, diced fine	
1 medium potato, diced fine	

1. In a 3-quart saucepan, combine the beans and water. Bring to a boil, boil rapidly for 2 minutes, remove from heat, and let stand an hour.

2. Pour the beans and their liquid into a large bowl. Dry out the saucepan and add the olive oil, onion, carrot, and potato. Sauté gently for about 15 minutes, stirring frequently, or until vegetables are tender.

3. Return the beans and their liquid to the saucepan. Add the chicken or meat broth, marjoram, salt, and pepper. Cover and simmer gently for about 2 hours or until beans are very tender.

4. Add the beet greens or frozen chopped spinach, return to a simmer and cook, uncovered, until beet greens are quite wilted or spinach is defrosted and soup has returned to serving temperature, about 15 minutes. (If desired, at this point, about half the soup may be pureed in a blender, food processor, or food mill or coarsely mashed with a wooden spoon or potato masher right in the pot.) Serve with thin slices of hard toasted Italian bread, a pepper mill, and a cruet of olive oil for enriching the soup to taste. *Makes 6 servings.*

Quick variation: Canned beans may be used in this soup with great success. Eliminate the bean soaking and begin recipe by sautéing vegetables. Add 3 20-ounce cans of cannellini beans with their liquid instead of the dried beans and cook 30 minutes instead of 2 hours. Proceed as above.

CURRIED ONION SOUP

This is a rice-thickened soup enriched with yogurt, excellent before broiled or roasted lamb or chicken.

1/2 cup rice
6 tablespoons butter
2 pounds onions, sliced thin
1 heaping tablespoon curry powder
1/4 teaspoon fresh-ground black pepper

5 cups chicken broth
1 cup plain yogurt
Salt to taste
Cracked or powdered coriander seed or cumin seed

1. Place the rice in a small bowl and cover with warm water. Let stand 1 hour.

2. In a 3-quart saucepan, melt the butter over medium heat and sauté the onions, curry powder, and pepper for 2 to 3 minutes.

3. Adjust heat to low. Drain the rice and add to the onion mixture. Cover and cook very slowly, stirring occasionally, until onions are very soft and rice has disintegrated, about 1-1/2 hours.

4. Stir in the chicken broth and simmer, covered, for 15 minutes. (May be prepared ahead to this point.)

5. Stir in the yogurt. Season with salt to taste. Heat through to serving temperature without returning to a boil. Garnish each bowl with a pinch of cracked or powdered coriander or cumin seed. *Makes 6 servings.*

A SPANISH-STYLE LENTIL SOUP

Another hearty legume soup. Serve this one with a salad and a cheese board for an informal, but satisfying, vegetarian supper.

1 large Spanish or Bermuda onion chopped fine
1 medium green pepper, seeded and chopped fine
1 small red pepper (or jarred pimiento), seeded and chopped fine
4 tablespoons olive oil
2 tablespoons flour

1 1-pound can plum tomatoes
4 carrots, scraped and chopped fine
1 tablespoon salt
1/4 teaspoon fresh-ground black pepper
1 pound lentils
2 quarts water

1. In a 5-quart saucepan, combine the chopped onion, green pepper, red pepper, and olive oil. Cook over low heat until vegetables are very soft, but not browned.

2. Stir in the flour and cook another 3 minutes without browning.

3. Stir in the tomatoes, carrots, salt, pepper, lentils, and water. Cover and simmer gently for about 2 hours, stirring occasionally. Correct seasoning. *Makes about 6 servings.*

HARRIET LEMBECK'S CARAWAY SOUP

This is a relatively easy soup to prepare, but as served to me by wine and food authority Harriet Lembeck, with a dollop of unsweetened whipped cream and a glass of iced aquavit (which also has a caraway flavor), it was most elegant. Use it to introduce a fine piece of roasted beef, a bouquet of buttered steamed vegetables, and Yorkshire pudding (see page 124). It would also be excellent before almost any dish with sauerkraut, such as choucroute garnie or bigos, the Polish hunter's stew (see page 78).

5 tablespoons butter
5 tablespoons flour
1-1/2 tablespoons caraway seeds
3 envelopes beef bouillon crystals
1-1/2 teaspoons salt
1/4 teaspoon fresh-ground black pepper

1 teaspoon sweet Hungarian paprika
1-1/2 quarts water
2 egg yolks
1/2 cup heavy cream, whipped

1. In a 3-quart saucepan, melt the butter over medium heat. Blend in flour, caraway seeds, bouillon crystals, salt, and pepper. Cook, stirring frequently, for 5 minutes. Be careful not to burn the mixture. Blend in paprika and remove from heat. Allow bubbling to subside.

2. Add the water, stirring constantly. Return to heat and bring to a simmer, still stirring constantly. Cover and simmer 15 minutes.

3. Strain the soup into a large bowl and discard caraway seeds. (Soup can be prepared in advance to this point.)

4. Just before serving, beat in egg yolks with a wire whisk, then return to saucepan and heat through to serving temperature without boiling. Correct seasoning. Serve garnished with a dollop of unsweetened whipped cream and a glass of iced aquavit or an imported vodka such as Stolichnaya (Russian), Wyborowa (Polish), or Izmira (Turkish). *Makes 6 servings.*

TURKISH VEGETABLE SOUP

With the orange of carrots, the pale green of celery, the deep green of spinach, and an egg-enriched yellow base, this soup is particularly beautiful. And without much fuss, its lemon and herb flavorings nicely dress up a meal of broiled or roasted chicken, lamb, even hamburgers.

3 tablespoons butter
1 carrot, diced fine or cut into
  1-inch julienne strips
1 rib celery, diced fine or cut into
  1-inch julienne strips
2-1/2 tablespoons flour
3 cups chicken broth
2 cups water
1 pound fresh spinach, chopped,

or 1 10-ounce package chopped
  spinach, defrosted
Salt to taste
Juice of 1 lemon
3 egg yolks
3 tablespoons chopped fresh dill
  or 1 tablespoon dried dill weed
2 tablespoons chopped parsley

1. In a large saucepan, melt the butter over medium heat and sauté carrot and celery for 2 minutes. Stir in flour and continue to cook over medium heat for 2 more minutes without browning the vegetables or flour. Remove from heat and allow bubbling to subside.

2. Blend in chicken broth and water, stirring constantly. Return to heat and simmer gently, uncovered, for 10 minutes.

3. Add the spinach, salt, and lemon juice. Continue to simmer slowly for 10 more minutes. (Soup may be prepared ahead to this point.)

4. Just before serving, beat in egg yolks with a wire whisk, stir in the dill and parsley. Heat through over low heat to serving temperature. Do not boil. *Makes 6 servings.*

LIME SOUP

This seems at first like nothing but chicken and rice soup, but it is infinitely more interesting. Serve it hot or cold with tortilla chips.

2 quarts chicken broth
1/2 cup rice
1/2 cup lime juice
Salt to taste

1 large avocado, peeled and diced
Crushed chili pepper or red
  pepper flakes
Tortilla chips

1. In a 3-quart saucepan, bring the chicken broth to a boil. Add rice gradually so broth does not stop boiling and simmer for about 15 minutes or until rice is tender.

2. Stir in the lime juice, heat through, and season with salt to taste.

3. Serve hot or well chilled with garnishes of diced avocado and crushed red pepper. Tortilla chips should be served on the side, but can be crumbled into the soup. *Makes 6 servings.*

CREAM OF BROCCOLI SOUP

This is a very simple and marvelously thick soup that is delicious either hot or cold. Even when served hot, however, it seems to taste better when made a day ahead.

6 cups chicken broth
1 bunch broccoli, cleaned and
  chopped coarse
1 large potato, diced
1 rib celery, chopped
1 small leek (white part only) or
  onion, chopped

1 bay leaf
Salt and fresh-ground black
  pepper to taste
1/2 cup heavy cream
Sour cream (optional)
Chopped chives (optional)

1. In a 3-quart saucepan, combine the broth, broccoli, potato, celery, leek or onion, and bay leaf. Bring to a simmer and cook, un-

covered, until the vegetables are very tender, about 35 minutes. Remove bay leaf.

2. Puree the soup in a blender, food processor, or food mill, then return to the saucepan. Check seasoning and add salt and pepper to taste. If puree is too thick, add a little more chicken broth.

3. Stir in the cream and heat through, if serving hot. If serving cold, stir in the cream, chill well, and make sure to correct seasoning just before serving. Either hot or cold, the soup may be garnished with a dollop of sour cream and sprinkling of chives. *Makes 6 servings.*

SPRING ONION AND RED POTATO SOUP

This is a variation on traditional French leek and potato soup.

2 bunches scallions (including all healthy-looking green part), chopped coarse
1-1/2 pounds unpeeled red new potatoes, scrubbed and cut in half

6 cups water
1 cup heavy cream
Salt and fresh ground black pepper to taste
Fine-chopped parsley or another fresh herb

1. In a 3-quart saucepan, combine the scallions, potatoes, and water. Cover and simmer until potatoes are very tender, about 30 minutes.

2. Puree the soup in a blender, food processor, or food mill, then return to the saucepan.

3. Return soup to a simmer for 3 minutes, stirring constantly. If serving hot, add the cream, salt, and pepper and heat through. If serving cold, add cream, chill well, and remember to correct seasoning just before serving. Garnish with chopped parsley or other herbs. *Makes 6 servings.*

GENOESE RICE AND BEAN SOUP

This is a soup to make when you've had your fill of pesto, the Genoese basil sauce (see page 42), on pasta. On a hot summer day, it's lovely served at room temperature.

1 small (about 1 pound) green
  cabbage, chopped coarse
1/2 pound fresh spinach, stemmed
  and chopped coarse, or 1/2 10-
  ounce box frozen chopped
  spinach
2 medium potatoes, peeled and
  diced
1 medium onion, chopped fine
2 tablespoons olive oil

6 cups water
1 teaspoon salt
1/4 teaspoon fresh-ground black
  pepper
1 20-ounce can cannellini beans,
  drained
1/2 cup rice
2 heaping tablespoons pesto sauce
  or more to taste
1/4 cup grated Parmesan cheese

1. In a 5- to 8-quart pot, combine the cabbage, spinach, potatoes, onion, oil, water, salt, and pepper. Bring to a simmer, partially cover, and simmer gently for an hour.

2. Add the canned beans and rice, stir well, then continue to simmer 15 minutes longer or until rice is tender.

3. Remove from heat, stir in pesto sauce and cheese, then correct salt and pepper. Let stand for at least 10 minutes before serving. If serving at room temperature, pour the soup into serving bowls and let it cool for at least an hour. It will become thick and stewlike. Soup may be served with additional cheese on the side. *Makes about 6 servings.*

CHICK-PEA AND SAUSAGE SOUP

The only course you would want after this substantial soup is an omelet or cheese board and salad.

3 tablespoons olive oil
1 large red onion, chopped
1/4 pound mushrooms, sliced thin
1 or 2 large cloves garlic, chopped
1 tablespoon chopped parsley
3/4 teaspoon rosemary, crumbled
   between the fingers
1 1-pound can plum tomatoes
   with their juice

2 16-ounce cans chick-peas,
   drained
1/2 teaspoon salt
1/4 teaspoon fresh-ground black
   pepper
1 pound sweet Italian sausage
6 cups water or beef broth
Fresh-grated Parmesan cheese

1. In a 5- to 8-quart casserole, combine the oil, onion, mushrooms, garlic, parsley, and rosemary. Cook over medium heat until vegetables are tender, about 15 minutes.

2. Add the tomatoes and their juice and break them up with a wooden spoon. Simmer for 15 minutes.

3. Add the chick-peas, salt, and pepper. Remove the sausage from its casing and let the meat drop into the pot in large pieces. Add the water or broth and bring to a simmer. Simmer, partially covered, for about 40 minutes. Serve cheese separately. *Makes about 6 servings.*

HARVEST SOUP

This sweet vegetable soup improves with reheating.

2 tablespoons butter
2 medium onions, sliced
1 quart beef broth
1 quart water
3 medium ripe tomatoes, chopped
   (no need to peel)
1 small winter squash, peeled and
   cut into 1/2-inch cubes

2 medium carrots, sliced
1 cup shelled lima beans (frozen
   will do)
2 ears of corn, stripped
1/2 pound string beans

1. In a 5- to 8-quart casserole, heat the butter and sauté the onions over medium heat until golden, about 15 minutes.

2. Add all the remaining ingredients, except corn and string beans, and simmer, uncovered, for 30 minutes.

3. Add the corn kernels and string beans and simmer another 30 minutes. *Makes 6 to 8 servings.*

SWEET AND SOUR CABBAGE SOUP

This is my grandmother's recipe which she got from her mother, who was from Minsk in Russia. If you can't find citric acid crystals — what my grandmother calls sour salt — for the authentic sour flavor, use about 7 tablespoons lemon juice or white vinegar. If you think everyone will like the sweet and sour soup meat — and I can't imagine not liking it — place a piece of it in each bowl. You can serve rye bread and a cheese board to complete the menu.

2 pounds beef flanken
3 quarts cold water
1 35-ounce can peeled plum tomatoes, chopped and with their juice
1 large head cabbage, shredded

1 tablespoon salt
1/2 teaspoon fresh-ground black pepper
1/2 cup sugar (or more)
1-3/4 teaspoons citric acid crystals (or more)

1. In a large pot, combine the beef flanken and cold water. Bring to a simmer over high heat, skimming off whatever foam rises to the top.

2. When foam has stopped rising, add the remaining ingredients and stir well. Simmer, with cover slightly askew, for at least 2 hours or until meat is falling off the bones.

3. Adjust the sweet and sour seasoning to taste by adding sugar and/ or citric acid. My grandmother describes the proper flavor as "winey." At any rate, it should be a reasonably rich flavor. It improves with reheating. *Makes 8 generous servings.*

SCHAV

Schav, which is Russian, is a summer staple in my parents' home, although they are American-born. It took many years before I acquired a taste for this refreshingly sour soup, but now I too make it in very large batches when sorrel is in season—in early summer, then again in early fall. It will keep for several weeks in the refrigerator, if you don't drink it up before that long. It is usually served with vegetable garnishes and sour cream, but I like to drink it without embellishment, out of a glass as a cooler after work or when I get home from the beach. Taken straight, it has no more calories than a green salad, so, for me, it is a guilt-free indulgence.

Sorrel is probably difficult to find in some parts of the country, but the seeds are not and it grows very well in a window box or clay pot. At any rate, you can make a similar soup with spinach by adding enough lemon juice to make it tarter.

3 pounds fresh sorrel	*Few drops lemon juice (optional)*
3 quarts cold water	*Sour cream*
Salt and fresh-ground black	*Chopped cucumber*
pepper to taste	*Chopped scallions*
3 eggs (optional)	

1. Pick over and wash the sorrel well. Remove the tough stems, then chop the leaves fine.

2. In a 5- to 8-quart enameled or stainless steel saucepan, bring the water to a rolling boil. Drop in the sorrel and boil for 10 minutes. Remove from heat. Season with salt and pepper to taste. Taste, and if a slightly tarter edge is desired, add a little lemon juice.

3. To enrich the soup with egg, in a small bowl beat the eggs well. Bring the soup to a boil, remove from heat, then beat the eggs into the hot soup. (Don't add eggs if you plan to store the soup longer than a week.)

4. Pour schav into clean quart jars and refrigerate. Serve very well chilled with, if desired, a dollop of sour cream or yogurt, chopped cucumber and scallions. *Makes about 10 servings.*

BLACK BEAN SOUP

Here's a hearty soup to feed a party crowd. For a buffet, serve it in hot cups with the garnishes in bowls for guests to add as they please.

1 pound black beans
3 quarts water
6 tablespoons butter or vegetable oil
2 ribs celery
3 medium onions, chopped fine
1 pound (approximately) smoked pork shoulder, smoked pork knuckles, or smoked ham hock
3 bay leaves

1/2 teaspoon fresh-ground black pepper
2 teaspoons salt
3/4 cup dry Madeira
Sieved hard-boiled eggs (whites and yolks separate)
Chopped onion
Chopped green pepper
Sour cream
Lemon and/or lime wedges

1. In a 5-quart saucepan, combine the beans and water. Bring to a boil and boil for 2 minutes. Remove from heat and let stand for 1 hour.

2. Add the butter or oil, vegetables, the smoked pork, bay leaves, and pepper. Simmer gently, uncovered, for about 1-1/2 hours. Add salt and continue to cook until beans are very tender, about another 30 minutes.

4. Remove the smoked pork and reserve. Discard the bay leaves. With a food mill, blender, or food processor, puree the beans, then return them to the pot.

5. Add the Madeira and bring to a simmer. Correct seasoning. If soup is too thick, add a little water. If preparing ahead, however, correct the consistency when reheating.

6. To serve soup buffet style, supply guests with mugs or hot cups

and spoons. Arrange the sieved egg yolk and whites, chopped onion, and green pepper on a serving dish. Place lemon wedges and sour cream in separate bowls. Supply serving spoons for the garnishes and sour cream. Lemon and lime wedges can be handled with the fingers. *Makes about 10 servings.*

Pasta

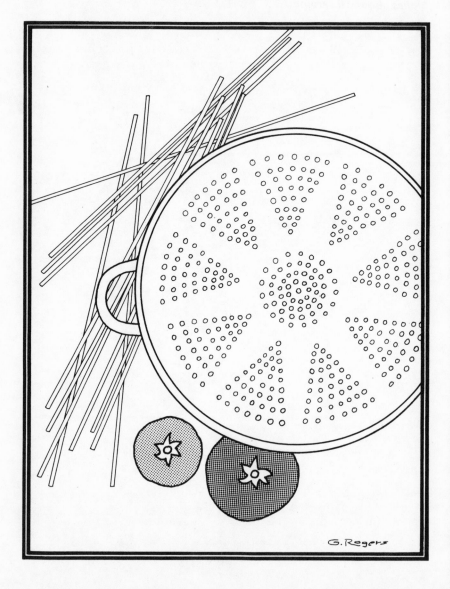

G. Rogers

Pasta is always served as a first course in Italy, but in this country we often eat pasta as the main course. The recipes here range from the simplest, most rustic, and perhaps most beloved pasta dish in Italy — *Aglio e olio* — to a fiery conglomeration of olives, capers, anchovies, and hot peppers that could easily be a main course with salad following. I'm afraid this chapter reflects my personal predilection for highly seasoned, even fiery food, but I've found all these recipes can be quickly and easily executed without requiring a great deal of preparation, valuable characteristics when you have little time or space to spare.

AGLIO E OLIO
(GARLIC AND OIL)

I can think of no greater comfort than aglio e olio when hunger attacks late at night, so this recipe serves only one. It is nothing to multiply the ingredients to taste.

1/4 cup olive oil
2 cloves garlic, chopped fine
1/4 pound spaghetti,
  linguine, or vermicelli

Salt and fresh-ground pepper
  to taste

1. Bring at least 6 cups of water with a heaping teaspoon of salt to a rolling boil.

2. Meanwhile, in a small skillet or saucepan, combine the oil and garlic. Set over low heat and cook until garlic is golden.

3. Cook the pasta, then drain in a strainer or colander. Immediately

place in a bowl and toss with hot oil. Season to taste with salt and pepper.

LINGUINE WITH CLAM SAUCE

The proper way to prepare clam sauce is to start with fresh clams. But if you can find cans of the tiny whole clams imported from Japan, you can knock out a satisfactory sauce in no time. Domestic chopped or minced clams in cans will do, too, but aren't as tender as the Japanese imports.

6 tablespoons olive oil
2 to 4 cloves garlic, chopped
   fine
1/4 cup fine-chopped parsley

1 8-ounce can whole baby
  clams
Salt to taste
1/2 pound linguine

1. In a small saucepan, combine the oil and garlic. Cook over medium-low heat until garlic is beginning to brown. Add the parsley and continue to cook until garlic is golden.

2. Drain the clam juice directly into the saucepan and simmer for 5 minutes. Set aside and just before the pasta is done, gently heat through with the whole clams. Do not cook the clams.

3. Boil the linguine in a minimum of 3 quarts of water with 2 teaspoons salt. Drain well. Divide between two bowls and top with clam sauce. *Makes 2 servings.*

MACARONI WITH GREEN SAUCE

A food processor is handy here for chopping the greens.

1/2 pound tubular macaroni
1-1/2 teaspoons salt
1/2 cup (1 stick) butter

3 scallions, chopped fine
  (including green part)

1 large clove garlic, chopped
fine
3 cups fine-chopped watercress or arugala (remove
only the tough stems)

1/2 cup fine-chopped fresh
parsley
Fresh-ground black pepper to
taste
Fresh-grated Parmesan cheese

1. Boil the macaroni in 3 quarts of boiling water with 2 teaspoons of salt. Begin sauce while macaroni cooks.

2. In a saucepan or skillet, melt the butter over medium heat. Add the scallions and garlic and sauté until scallions are limp.

3. Add the chopped watercress or arugala and the parsley. Continue to sauté over medium heat, stirring and tossing constantly, until greens are totally limp, 4 or 5 minutes.

4. Drain macaroni and pour into a serving bowl. Toss with the hot sauce and serve immediately with pepper and cheese. *Makes 2 servings.*

SPAGHETTI CARBONARA

Although a Roman specialty, this pasta dish is now served all over Italy and is fashionable in America, too. It is one of the few pasta dishes I find satisfying as a main course with only a big salad afterward.

1/2 to 3/4 pound sliced bacon,
cut into 1-inch pieces
2 tablespoons butter
4 eggs
3/4 cup fresh-grated Romano
or Parmesan cheese

1/2 teaspoon fresh-ground
black pepper
1 pound spaghetti or linguine
6 quarts water
1 tablespoon salt

1. In a skillet, sauté the bacon with the butter over medium heat until bacon is crisp.

2. Meanwhile, in a large serving bowl, beat the eggs until well mixed, then beat in the cheese and pepper.

3. Boil the spaghetti in 6 quarts of water with 1 tablespoon salt. Drain and return spaghetti to the hot pot.

4. Pour over the bacon and all the fat in the pan. Toss well. Pour over the egg and cheese mixture and toss well, correcting salt and pepper if necessary. Place in the large serving bowl and serve immediately. *Makes 4 servings.*

LINGUINE WITH TUNA AND HERB SAUCE

*3 scallions, chopped fine
(including green part)
1 large clove garlic (or more
to taste), chopped fine
3 tablespoons olive oil
1 teaspoon dried marjoram
Pinch dried thyme*

*1/4 cup fine-chopped fresh
parsley
1 cup dry white wine
2 7-ounce cans tuna, drained
Fresh-ground pepper to taste
1 pound linguine*

1. In a small saucepan, combine the scallions, garlic, and olive oil. Cook over medium heat until scallions are just limp.

2. Add the marjoram, thyme and parsley. Continue to cook for a few minutes. Add the wine. Bring to a simmer and simmer gently for about 2 minutes.

3. Add the tuna and season with pepper to taste. Simmer 5 minutes. Remove from heat.

4. Bring at least 6 quarts of water with a tablespoon of salt to a rolling boil. Add linguine and cook until al dente.

5. While pasta is cooking, reheat sauce until just bubbling. Drain pasta in a colander and immediately toss in a bowl with the sauce. Serve immediately without cheese. *Makes 4 to 6 servings.*

SPAGHETTI ALL'AMATRICIANA

In the style of Amatrice (a town in the Lazio region of Italy), says the name of the dish, yet I learned this version of it from Giacomo Cora, a Milanese wine shipper.

6 or more quarts of water	1 1-pound can plum tomatoes,
8 slices bacon, diced	drained
3 tablespoons butter	Salt
1 small onion, chopped fine	1 pound spaghetti
1 chili pepper, halved and	Fresh-grated Romano cheese
seeded	(about 1 cup)

1. Bring at least 6 quarts of water with 1 tablespoon salt to a rolling boil.

2. Meanwhile, in a skillet, combine the bacon and butter and cook over medium heat until bacon is about half-cooked.

3. Add the onion and pepper and continue to cook until onion is wilted. Add the tomatoes and break them up with a wooden spoon.

4. Put the pasta on to boil.

5. Increase the heat and sauté tomatoes, seasoning with salt if necessary, for 10 minutes or until they are saucey.

6. When pasta is done, drain in a colander. Immediately toss in a bowl with the sauce and about 6 tablespoons cheese. Serve more cheese separately. *Makes 4 to 6 servings.*

DITALI WITH WILD MUSHROOMS AND HOT PEPPERS

This is a full-flavored but plainly dressed tubular macaroni to have before a robust main course of grilled meat or poultry.

1 ounce dried Italian funghi	1/2 cup olive oil
porcini (wild mushrooms)	2 cloves garlic
Warm water	1 or 2 whole chili peppers

1 pound ditali or other medium-sized tubular macaroni	2 tablespoons fine-chopped parsley

1. In a small bowl or cup, cover dried mushrooms with warm water and let stand 20 minutes.

2. Meanwhile, put up salted water for the macaroni and, in a small saucepan, heat the oil over medium heat. With the side of a wide knife, or the bottom of a heavy tumbler, smash the garlic cloves. Remove skin and add garlic to oil. Add pepper to oil. Cook until the garlic is browned but not at all burned. Remove both garlic and pepper.

3. Put the macaroni on to boil.

4. While the pasta and garlic and pepper are cooking, drain the mushrooms. Reserve the liquid in the freezer or refrigerator for another use (put it in a stew or soup or use it to make a sauce from the scraped up browned bits left from pan-broiling hamburgers). Chop the mushrooms coarse.

5. Add mushrooms and parsley to oil and sauté for 2 minutes.

6. Drain the macaroni in a colander and toss immediately into a bowl with the hot flavored oil and salt to taste. Serve immediately without grated cheese. *Makes 4 to 6 servings.*

SPAGHETTI FURIOSO

There are many versions of pasta with "furious sauce," and, as the name implies, they all contain a fair amount of hot pepper. Use whole dried peppers if possible and dried pepper flakes only if that is all you can find. And don't concern yourself about neatly pitting the olives. Just cut the flesh away from the pits roughly.

4 tablespoons olive oil	2 ribs celery, chopped coarse
1 medium onion, chopped coarse	2 cloves garlic, chopped coarse

1 1-pound can plum tomatoes
1/2 teaspoon fresh-ground
   black pepper
4 to 6 (to taste) dried hot
   cherry or chili peppers,
   seeded and crushed
1-1/2 teaspoons oregano
8 anchovy fillets, chopped
1/2 cup Sicilian green olives,
   pitted and cut up

1/2 cup oil-cured black
   olives, pitted and cut up
2 tablespoons capers
Salt to taste
1-1/2 pounds spaghetti
8 quarts water
1 tablespoon salt

1. In a large skillet, heat oil and sauté onion and celery over medium heat until tender.

2. Add garlic, tomatoes, black and red pepper, and oregano. With a wooden spoon, break up the tomatoes into small pieces. Increase heat slightly and cook rapidly for 10 minutes, stirring often.

3. Add the anchovies, olives, and capers. Mix well and continue to cook 3 or 4 more minutes. Add salt to taste.

4. Boil spaghetti in 8 quarts of boiling water with at least 1 table-spoon of salt. Drain well, place on a platter and top with sauce. Serve without cheese. *Makes 6 servings.*

LINGUINE CAVALRY STYLE

This treatment of butter, eggs, nuts, and cheese is even better on fresh egg pasta if you can get some.

1/2 cup (1 stick) butter, at
   room temperature
4 eggs
1-1/2 cups fresh-grated
   Parmesan cheese
1-1/2 cups walnuts, ground
1 teaspoon salt

1/2 teaspoon fresh-ground
   black pepper
1-1/2 pounds linguine (or
   fresh fettuccine)
8 quarts water
2 tablespoons salt

1. In a large serving bowl, cream together the butter, eggs, and cheese. Stir in the ground nuts, then season with salt and pepper.

2. Boil the linguine in 8 quarts of boiling water with 2 tablespoons of salt. Drain well, then pour into the butter mixture and toss well. Serve immediately with a pepper mill to add pepper to taste. Extra cheese is not usually necessary. *Makes 6 servings.*

PESTO

This is the most famous recipe of Genoa. A raw pasta sauce of pounded basil, garlic, oil, cheese, and often nuts, it is most commonly used on pasta, potatoes (in Genoa the two are even combined), and in soups (see page 28). A dollop of pesto on a broiled steak or piece of fish is also delicious.

Its name refers to the pestle with which the sauce is traditionally pounded, but a blender or food processor makes an equally good-tasting sauce, although not one with the exact same texture. The important thing is fresh basil, which, if you cannot purchase it from the grocer, is easy to grow in a flowerpot in a sunny window. When you finally do get fresh basil, make as much pesto as you can. Made without the cheese and stored in a jar with a quarter-inch of olive oil on top, it will keep perfectly until the next year's crop is in. The following recipe uses a little parsley with the basil so the sauce keeps a greener color, and it calls for less oil than many recipes because I like to toss the pasta with some butter as well. The recipe makes enough sauce to dress generously about 1-1/2 pounds of pasta or at least 6 servings.

2 cups (tightly packed) basil leaves
1/4 cup (tightly packed) parsley (remove tough stems)
3/4 cup olive oil
2 large cloves garlic, chopped coarse

1-1/2 tablespoons pignoli nuts (pine nuts) or walnuts
1/2 teaspoon salt
1/4 teaspoon fresh-ground black pepper
1 cup grated Romano, Sardo, or Parmesan cheese (or combination)

1. If using a blender, combine half the basil leaves, the parsley, half the olive oil, all the garlic, and all the nuts. Process on low speed, turning the motor on and off and pushing the leaves down into the blades, until chopped fine.

2. Add the remaining basil, olive oil, salt, and pepper. Continue processing until mixture is a fine paste. If using immediately, pour the pesto into a mixing bowl and stir in the cheese. Otherwise, pour into a wide-mouthed jar or plastic container and cover with about 1/4 inch olive oil. Spoon off this oil before using the pesto.

3. If using a food processor, combine all the ingredients in the bowl, except cheese. Process, turning the machine on and off at first, until mixture is a fine paste. Blend in cheese only if using immediately. *Makes 6 servings.*

4. To serve pasta with pesto, cook 1-1/2 pounds pasta as usual in salted boiling water. Meanwhile, place the pesto in a large serving bowl with 6 tablespoons of butter. Just before pasta is done, spoon 6 table-spoons of the boiling pasta water for each 4 into the pesto. Drain pasta and toss well with the sauce and butter. Correct salt and pepper as necessary and serve immediately. (For individual 4-ounce serving use about 1 heaping tablespoon pesto.)

Salads and Raw Foods

By their nature, salads and raw foods require little if any cooking. It's more assembly work. The washing, drying, peeling, trimming, slicing, chopping and other preparation of ingredients does require space, however. One piece of equipment that is well worth having in this respect is a plastic salad spinner-dryer. It operates on centrifugal force, spinning salad greens in a plastic colander that has been inserted into a solid plastic container, which collects the water spun off. I also use the outside section as a salad washing bowl and the inside as a separate colander even though they were not designed for it. Directions for doing this are outlined below. Collapsible wire salad drying baskets, which you have to spin around or shake with your arm, are easy to store but not as easy to use. And unless you don't mind getting everything a little damp, they have to be used in the bathroom or in the hall or outdoors. You can also dry salad, albeit cumbersomely, by gathering it in a large bath towel and shaking it sharply.

Many of the following salads have multiple uses — as appetizers for parties, formal first courses, side dishes, main courses for lunch, dinner, or brunch, buffet dishes, and snacks. They cover all kinds of seasonal produce as well as foods that are available throughout the year. With most everyone interested in their health and figures and consequently lighter food, main course salads are no longer just summer fare. It is indeed even fashionable to serve them all year.

How to Prepare Both Green and Mixed Salads

The typical American salad consists of lettuce, usually iceberg, tomatoes, generally tasteless, and cucumber, too often served with waxed skin. A gloppy dressing overpowers the whole thing, which, it must be said, is just as well.

Considering the many alternatives it is rather shameful that these ingredients have become the standard. Romaine and Boston lettuces are now widely available in supermarkets. Watercress, endive, curly chicory, and fresh spinach are more easily found than they used to be. Cherry tomatoes can substitute for salad tomatoes when salad tomatoes are out of season. Fennel bulbs (which have a sort of licorice flavor), red and white radishes, carrots, raw zucchini and asparagus, celery, beansprouts—almost any vegetable can be put in the salad bowl. When salad is the only vegetable dish being served, use a number of these. When there are other vegetables on the menu, all you may want is a bowl of mixed greens.

Rich, creamy dressings with cheese, sour cream, or mayonnaise have their place, I suppose, but most of the time the only dressing a salad needs is the best quality olive oil and wine vinegar you can find. Salt and fresh-ground pepper are the basic seasonings, but the judicious addition of strong mustard, fresh or dried herbs, chopped garlic, onion, shallots, capers, or anchovies can help you vary the flavor of the dressing from day to day.

The most important things to remember when making a salad of any kind are:

1. *Wash the vegetables and greens carefully.*
2. *Dry the vegetables and greens thoroughly.*
3. *Dress the salad immediately before serving, no sooner.*

It is hard to imagine anything more unappetizing than a gritty, gooey, wet, and wilted salad.

To wash salad greens in a plastic spinner dryer, remove the colander bowl and place the salad ingredients in the outside bowl. Fill the washing bowl with cold water and agitate the greens with your hand to rinse off dirt and sand. Do not drain off the water: you will be mixing the sand and the salad again if you do.

Remove the greens from the water with one hand and place in the colander bowl to drain. (If you have no drain board next to the sink, you will have to hold the colander over the sink with the other hand. This means you will have to work one-handed from now on.) Pour the dirty water down the drain, rinse out the bowl, and repeat washing at least one more time or until the salad is thoroughly cleaned.

To dry the salad, place the colander bowl back in the outside bowl, put on spinner cover and spin. Remove colander and drain outside bowl. Replace and spin again.

If preparing the salad ahead, place in a bowl lined with paper toweling. Refrigerate, covered with plastic, if not serving within 30 minutes. Remove from refrigerator about 15 minutes before serving. The salad should not be chilly, just cool.

OIL AND VINEGAR DRESSING

Proportions for salad dressing are so much a matter of taste and the quality of ingredients used that it is difficult to give a specific recipe. Oils with a strong flavor may stand for more vinegar than bland oils will. A potent vinegar may have to be used more judiciously than a dilute one. The general rule of thumb, however, is one part vinegar to three parts oil. Start with this ratio and adjust to taste. For an average salad for two, this ratio can be taken as:

3 tablespoons olive oil   *Fresh-ground pepper to taste*
1/2 teaspoon salt
1 tablespoon red-wine or sherry
   vinegar

1. To mix the dressing separately, in a cup or small bowl, dissolve the salt in the vinegar, using a table fork or whisk, then beat in the oil. Pepper is best added to the salad itself.

2. To mix the dressing on the salad, toss the salad gently with the olive oil. Place the salt in a large soupspoon, then pour the vinegar into

the spoon. Holding the spoon over the salad and using a fork, stir the salt into the vinegar, letting drops of vinegar fall into the salad. When the salt is dissolved, pour the remaining vinegar into the salad. Grind in pepper to taste, then toss gently, but thoroughly.

Variations: For the above amount of dressing, add from a drop to a heaping 1/4 teaspoon of Dijon mustard, a pinch of dried herbs of any kind, fine-chopped garlic, shallots, or onion to taste, chopped or whole capers, one or two fine-chopped or mashed anchovy fillets. Lemon juice or cider or malt vinegar can be substituted for the wine or sherry vinegar. Walnut oil can be substituted for the olive oil.

SPINACH AND MUSHROOM SALAD

There are many variations on the spinach and mushroom theme. One I particularly like is made with a dressing of walnut oil, lemon juice, broken walnuts, and fresh chives with a few of the purple chive flowers if you grow your own. The following recipe and variations, though, are made with the more conventional bacon dressing.

1 pound fresh spinach	*3 tablespoons red-wine vinegar*
1/3 pound mushrooms, sliced thin	*Fresh-ground pepper to taste*
1/2 pound bacon, cut into batons	
or 1/2-inch pieces	

1. To remove the tough stems, fold the spinach leaves in half down the stem. Hold the leaf folded between thumb and first finger of left hand. Pull stem off with right hand. Wash and dry the spinach well, then place in a salad bowl. Place mushrooms on top.

2. In a skillet, cook the bacon until crisp. For a wilted salad, pour in the vinegar and remove from heat immediately. Pour contents of skillet on the salad immediately and toss. If you want the spinach to remain crisp, remove crisped bacon and drain on absorbent paper. Add vinegar to bacon fat and allow to cool before tossing with salad and drained bacon. Season with pepper and toss well. *Makes 2 or 3 servings.*

Variation: To make a creamy dressing, beat in a small bowl an egg yolk with 1/4 teaspoon of Dijon mustard. When bacon is crisp, remove to absorbent paper. Then, with a whisk or fork, beat warm bacon fat very, very slowly into the beaten egg. Season with vinegar or lemon juice, fresh-ground pepper and salt if necessary.

CAESAR SALAD

Caesar Cardini, who owned a small restaurant in Tijuana in the 1920s, invented this salad and named it after himself. Caesar's Place was one of the more popular haunts of Hollywood stars, and during the long July 4 weekend in 1924, so the story goes, Cardini ran out of food. All that was left in the kitchen were crates of romaine lettuce, eggs, Romano cheese, and such staples as bread, oil, and lemons.

In a moment of inspiration, Cardini who had been a salad man in his earlier days, assembled the serving staff and had them arrange all the serving carts available with wooden salad bowls, pepper mills, cheese graters, and bowls of fresh, crisp croutons. By making the preparation of his make-do salad into a showy performance, he supposedly fooled his clientele into thinking they were getting something quite special. The following is not quite the original recipe — anchovies seem to have been added later and Cardini supposedly used garlic-flavored oil rather than whole garlic.

1 clove garlic	1 coddled egg (see note)
1/2 teaspoon salt	Juice of 1/2 lemon
1/4 teaspoon Worcestershire sauce	1 large or 2 small heads romaine
1-1/2 teaspoons red-wine vinegar	lettuce, washed and dried
2 tablespoons olive oil	1/3 cup grated Romano or Par-
3 to 4 anchovy fillets	mesan cheese
1/3 cup olive oil	1/2 cup croutons

1. In a salad bowl, with a fork, crush the garlic and salt together. Add the Worcestershire sauce, vinegar, 2 tablespoons oil, and ancho-

vies. Continue to mash and stir with fork until mixture is homogenous.

2. With the fork, beat in the remaining oil, then break in the coddled egg, then lemon juice to taste.

3. Break the romaine into the bowl in 2-inch pieces. Toss gently.
Add the grated cheese and croutons. Toss gently but thoroughly.
Serve immediately. *Makes 2 generous servings.*

Note: To make a coddled egg, place an unshelled egg in a small
saucepan of boiling water. Turn off the heat and let stand 1 minute.

RICE SALADS

Boiled rice makes a good base for salad, and whenever you have left-
over rice you should store it in the refrigerator already dressed with
oil and vinegar (or lemon juice) so it is ready to be combined with
whatever you have in mind to put in it. Almost any diced vegetable or
meat leftovers will do. Use this salad as a first course or part of an
antipasto assortment. You can, of course, also boil rice specifically for
a salad.

1-1/2 cups raw white rice
2 quarts or more boiling salted
  water
3 tablespoons olive oil
2 to 3 tablespoons wine vinegar
2 medium carrots, chopped fine
1 small onion, chopped fine

1 small green pepper, chopped
  fine
1 large rib celery, chopped fine
1/4 cup fine-chopped parsley
Salt and fresh-ground pepper to
  taste

1. In a 3-quart saucepan, boil the rice in salted water for about 15
minutes or until tender, but not soft. Drain immediately and thoroughly in a colander or strainer.

2. In a salad or serving bowl, toss the hot rice with oil and vinegar.
Add the remaining ingredients and toss well. Refrigerate until chilled
or ready to serve. Correct seasoning before serving. *Makes 6 servings.*

Variation: To make the above salad substantial enough for a main course, add 1 7-ounce can tuna, flaked; 8 large green olives (preferably Spanish or Sicilian), chopped; 1/4 pound Provolone cheese, cut into small cubes and 2 to 3 tomatoes, chopped fine.

BROCCOLI AND ANCHOVY SALAD

A good antipasto all by itself, this salad is also an excellent side dish with veal piccata (page 108).

1 bunch broccoli	*1 to 2 tablespoons wine vinegar*
1/2 2-ounce can anchovy fillets	*Fresh-ground pepper to taste*
3 tablespoons olive oil	

1. Trim off leaves and break the broccoli into flowerets. Wash thoroughly. Steam or boil until barely tender. It should still be a very bright green.
2. Drain in a colander, then run under cold water until cooled to room temperature.
3. Arrange the broccoli in a bowl, then, working right over the salad bowl, cut each anchovy fillet into three or four pieces.
4. In a small bowl or cup, beat the oil and vinegar together. Pour dressing over broccoli, grind on pepper to taste and serve. This salad does not have to be served immediately. It can wait at room temperature for several hours. *Makes 4 servings.*

SWEET AND SOUR WILTED SALAD

In the American Midwest, wilted salad is most often made with leaf or garden lettuce or dandelion leaves, but spinach (see spinach and mushroom salad, page 48) and escarole also make good wilted salads.

1 large head leaf or garden lettuce, 1 bunch dandelion greens,
1 pound spinach, or 1 small
head escarole
1/2 pound sliced bacon, cut into
1/2-inch pieces

1 medium onion, chopped
3 tablespoons cider vinegar
1 to 1-1/2 tablespoons sugar

1. Wash, dry, and tear into pieces the lettuce or other greens.

2. In a skillet, fry the bacon over medium heat. When almost crisp, add the chopped onion.

3. When the bacon is crisp, add the cider vinegar and sugar. Stir for 1 minute, then immediately pour over prepared salad greens. Serve immediately. *Makes 4 servings.*

SALAD WITH BATONS OF BACON AND EGGS MOLLET

It wasn't too long ago that this salad, or at least one very like it, was the rage at a very chic Paris restaurant-cum-disco where a six-ounce Coke on ice costs $6. Everyone (and supposedly Everyone in the fashion world eats there) seemed to be ordering it as a first course.

However, since that first encounter, I have eaten very similar salads at many French restaurants, as first courses and main ones, indicating that the rage has spread and it is no longer chic, just delicious.

It is probably one of the more difficult recipes in this book because it needs careful timing and coordination. Eggs mollet have runny or soft yolks with firm whites. It also requires using more utensils than usual. But it adapts well to being done in stages a little ahead of time and it is one of my favorite light suppers. I've also served it with success for brunch. Either way you must accompany it with garlic toast (see note), something they had too much snobbery and not enough imagination to serve at that Paris night spot.

1 small head leaf lettuce
2 medium heads endive
1 bunch watercress or arugala
   (rocket, a peppery salad green)
1/4 pound slab bacon
2 quarts water
4 eggs
1-1/2 tablespoons red-wine
   vinegar

Heaping 1/4 teaspoon Dijon
   mustard
1/2 teaspoon salt
1/4 cup olive oil
Fresh-ground black pepper to
   taste

1. Separate the leaf lettuce and endive leaves and cut off any thick stems from the watercress or arugala. Wash and dry all very well. (If preparing ahead, layer greens between sheets of paper toweling and store in bottom of refrigerator or in vegetable crisper. Remove about 20 minutes before assembling salad.)

2. Cut the bacon into baton-shaped pieces about 1 inch long and 1/8 inch on each side. Place in a cold skillet large enough to hold the bacon in one layer. Fry slowly until quite a bit of the fat has rendered off. Raise heat slightly and fry until crisp. Remove bacon with a slotted spoon and drain on absorbent paper. (This may be done well ahead of time, even a day or so. Store, wrapped in paper toweling, in a tin or jar. Do not refrigerate.)

3. To make eggs mollet, bring 2 quarts of water to a rolling boil. Meanwhile, with a pin or tack, make a 1/4- to 3/8-inch puncture in the large end of each egg. Place them in the boiling water and immediately adjust heat so that water is just below the simmering point. Time eggs for 7 minutes.

4. Immediately drain the eggs and run them under cold water until cool enough to handle. Carefully crack and peel eggs, remembering that the yolks are still soft. (Eggs may be peeled up to an hour ahead. Set aside in a glass or plastic container filled with cool water. Do not refrigerate).

5. To prepare dressing, in a small bowl or cup, with a fork, beat together the vinegar, mustard, and salt. Then, gradually beat in the oil until well blended.

6. To assemble and serve salad, toss the greens with the bits of bacon and dressing. Arrange the salad on two plates and place two

whole eggs on top of each serving. Each diner breaks into the egg, releasing the runny yolk, which becomes a sort of addition to the salad dressing. Serve with a pepper mill for pepper to be added to taste. *Makes 4 servings.*

Note: To make garlic toast, place 1/2-inch-thick slices of Italian or French bread under the broiler until they are toasted on both sides. While they are still hot, rub them with a clove of garlic. The more you rub, the stronger the garlic taste will be. Arrange the toasts on a serving plate and drizzle generously with olive oil; sprinkle with salt and fresh-ground pepper to taste.

ENDIVE ANTIPASTO SALAD

The idea for this came from another chic restaurant, this one in New York's SoHo artist district, where in order to partake of the so-called Bohemian life one must be selling one's creations for five figures. At any rate, I refused to pay this restaurant's price for a salad that, even if made with relatively expensive ingredients, seemed ridiculously easy to prepare.

It ends up to be a very versatile salad, too. With bread and a hearty red wine it is a complete lunch for four. It will serve six as a first course in an informal meal where the main course is soup or pasta. It can also be served as the antipasto on a more formal menu or as part of a cold buffet.

1 small onion
4 large heads Belgian endive
1/4 pound thin-sliced mortadella (preferably imported)
1/4 pound thin-sliced mortadella (preferably imported)
1/4 pound thin-sliced Switzerland Swiss or Gruyère cheese
5 to 6 red radishes

Scant 1/2 teaspoon salt
1-1/2 tablespoons red-wine vinegar
5 tablespoons olive oil
1/4 cup fine-chopped parsley
12 Black or Greek olives (or more)
Fresh-ground black pepper to taste

1. Cut the onion in half through the root end. Cut out the root. Then cut each half into thin crescents through the root end. Soak in cold water to cover for 30 minutes.

2. Cut the endive lengthwise into eighths and separate all the leaves by cutting out the core. Rinse and dry well. Arrange a bed of the leaves on a serving platter.

3. Cut through the stacks of sliced salami, mortadella, and cheese, slicing them all into 1/4-inch wide strips. Scatter these over the endive, mixing them all together.

4. Drain the onion, dry well, and scatter the slices over the salad. Cut the radishes into thin rounds and scatter these over the salad.

5. In a small bowl or cup, dissolve the salt in the vinegar, then beat in the oil and parsley. Pour over the salad and serve within several hours. Garnish with olives, serve with a pepper mill. Toss the salad at the table.

EGG NOODLE SALAD WITH TUNA AND CHEESE

The day this recipe was kitchen-tested, I packed the tossed noodles and various garnishes in separate plastic containers and bags and took it all to Central Park for a concert. With a jug of wine and several bags of fresh summer fruits for dessert, it was a memorable picnic for four. To make the meal more elaborate, you might also pour cold crab bisque (see page 14) into a thermos bottle and take it along.

This salad is an excellent cold appetizer as well, to serve six before broiled fish.

8 ounces fine egg noodles (preferably long Italian type)
6 tablespoons olive oil
1 large clove garlic, chopped fine

1-1/2 tablespoons fine-chopped fresh basil or parsley
1/3 cup sliced imported sour gherkin pickles (cornichons)

1 medium green pepper, seeded
and diced
1/2 cup chopped pickled
mushrooms
Salt and fresh-ground pepper to
taste
1 to 2 teaspoons red wine vinegar
Lettuce

1 6-1/2- or 7-ounce can tuna,
drained
6 ounces Gruyère, Swiss, or imported Provolone cheese, cut
into thin strips
Fresh plum tomatoes or sliced
tomatoes

1. Cook noodles in boiling salted water until just tender. If fresh
noodles, they should be done only a minute after the water returns
to the boil. Dried noodles will take longer: consult package directions.

2. Drain noodles in a colander, then run under cold water. Shake
noodles in colander to remove as much water as possible.

3. In a small saucepan or skillet, heat the olive oil over low heat.
Add garlic and sauté until lightly browned. Add basil or parsley, stir
a few times over heat, then remove from heat and allow to cool
slightly.

4. In a large mixing bowl, combine the noodles, oil mixture, gherkins, green pepper, and mushrooms. Toss, then refrigerate until 20 to
30 minutes before serving.

5. Before serving, correct for seasoning, adding more vinegar as well
as salt and pepper, if necessary. Arrange noodles in a mound on a bed
of lettuce in the center of a serving platter. Arrange chunks of tuna,
cheese, and tomatoes on platter. Allow each person to mix the cheese
and tuna into the noodle base to taste. *Makes 4 light main-course or 6
first-course servings*

CHICKEN AND AVOCADO SALAD

The easiest way to cook chicken for a salad, or any time you need
cooked chicken meat, is to poach boned chicken breasts in a well-
flavored broth. I realize that meat from a cooked whole chicken is
somewhat more flavorful. But considering that almost all chicken to-

day is relatively flavorless anyway, I don't see that it matters much.

If you flavor the broth well, it will help. And if you poach the chicken cutlets in one layer in a skillet, you won't have to use too much broth to improve the flavor:

In a skillet just large enough to hold the cutlets, combine about 1-1/2 cups canned chicken broth, 1/4 cup dry vermouth or white wine, 1 sliced carrot, 1 sliced medium onion, a few peppercorns, and a bay leaf. Cover and boil together for about 10 minutes.

Arrange the chicken cutlets in the skillet and add a little more broth, if necessary, so the chicken is just covered with broth. Adjust heat so that liquid quietly simmers for 5 minutes. Remove from heat and let cool in the broth for 5 minutes. Remove chicken and strain broth. Broth may be used again if kept frozen or if refrigerated and brought to a simmer every other day.

Put this particular chicken salad on a bed of fresh spinach or pile it into the scooped-out avocado shells, serve with hot cornbread and a chilled Riesling. With fresh fruit for dessert this should be a very satisfying lunch, but you can precede it with a soup.

1 cup mayonnaise
1 bunch watercress
3 scallions (including green
   part)
1/2 teaspoon dried tarragon,
   crushed
2 ripe avocados

1/2 lemon
1 pound cooked chicken breasts,
   cubed
Salt and fresh-ground black
   pepper to taste
Sprigs of watercress

1. In a blender or food processor, combine the mayonnaise, watercress, scallions, parsley, and tarragon. Blend to finely chop all the ingredients. Set aside.

2. Cut the avocados in half and remove the pits. Immediately squeeze a little lemon juice on the avocado pulp to prevent it from discoloring. With a spoon, scoop most of the avocado pulp out of the shells and into a large bowl, trying to keep the pulp in large pieces.

(Leave a thin lining of pulp in the shells if you plan to refill them.) Sprinkle the pulp (and the insides of the shells) with lemon juice.

3. Cut the scooped-out pulp into half-inch chunks. Add the mayonnaise and chicken. Mix together and season to taste with salt and pepper.

4. Pile the salad in the avocado shells. Chill but do not serve very cold. Garnish each with a sprig of watercress. Serve with hot corn bread or spoon bread. *Makes 2 main course servings.*

GADO GADO

This is not an authentic Indonesian recipe, yet the feeling of the dish is certainly exotic to most tastes. I can't recommend it highly enough. It is always a success. If you prepare the sauce and cut all the vegetables ahead of time, there is only a minor effort at the last minute. If the potatoes are cut ahead, however, store them, covered with water with a few drops of lemon juice, in the refrigerator, to prevent them from discoloring.

2 large potatoes, peeled and cut into 1/2-inch cubes
1/2 cup water
3 medium carrots, sliced thin
1/2 pound string beans, cut into inch-long pieces
1 cup shredded cabbage
1 cup mung bean sprouts
1 medium cucumber, diced
1 small green pepper, seeded and diced
4 hard-cooked eggs, each cut in half lengthwise

For sauce:
6 tablespoons 100% natural peanut butter
2 teaspoons molasses
1 large clove garlic, crushed
1 teaspoon cayenne pepper
1 to 1-1/2 cups beef broth
1/2 teaspoon salt
1 teaspoon lemon juice

1. In a 3-quart saucepan, combine the potatoes and water. Cover and simmer for about 3 minutes.

2. Add the carrots and stringbeans. Cover and simmer 2 minutes.

3. Add the cabbage and simmer another 5 minutes. Drain well.

4. On a large platter, arrange a bed of the steamed vegetables. In a decorative pattern, arrange the remaining vegetables — the raw bean sprouts, diced cucumber, and green pepper — on top of the steamed ones. Arrange the egg halves in the center or on the outer-edge. Serve with peanut butter sauce.

5. To make sauce, in a small saucepan combine all the sauce ingredients and, stirring constantly, bring to a simmer. (If you must use a commercial peanut butter with added oil and such, use less liquid.) The sauce should be thick, but pourable. Remove from heat and serve warm. *Makes 4 servings.*

Note: To use the rest of the head of cabbage, shred and mix with mayonnaise for coleslaw or steam until tender with butter and only the water that clings to it after washing.

FATOOSH (LEBANESE BREAD SALAD)

A bread-based salad, this is a relative of the Spanish bread-thickened cold vegetable soup, gazpacho. The word *gazpacho* derives from an Arabic word meaning "soaked bread." Serve fatoosh as a light meal by itself, as an appetizer, or as an accompaniment to broiled red meat or Italian sausage.

2 6-inch loaves pita or "Syrian"
bread
Cold water
1/2 head iceberg lettuce
2 medium ripe tomatoes, cut into
1/4-inch cubes
1 medium cucumber, cut into
1/4-inch cubes
1 medium onion, chopped

1/3 cup olive oil
2 to 3 tablespoons fresh lemon
juice (1 to 1-1/2 lemons)
Salt and fresh-ground black pep-
per to taste
3 tablespoons fine-chopped
fresh mint leaves or 1 table-
spoon crushed dried mint leaves

1. Split each pita loaf to make two full round halves. Place them all on a plate and sprinkle generously with water to moisten, but not soak, them. Set aside

2. Core the lettuce, wash well, then dry thoroughly. Cut in small pieces.

3. Tear the pita bread into 1/2-inch pieces and place in a large salad bowl. Add the lettuce, tomatoes, cucumber, and onion. Toss lightly.

4. Drizzle on the olive oil and lemon juice. Season with salt and pepper. Add the mint. Toss again. Cover and refrigerate for about an hour. Toss again and serve slightly chilled. *Serves 3 to 4 as an appetizer or a side dish.*

TABOULEH (BULGUR WHEAT AND PARSLEY SALAD)

I make tabouleh salad all summer long, in very large batches, because it is one of the most refreshing dishes in existence and it remains delicious even after several days of refrigerator storage. I am apt, in fact, to simply stand by the open refrigerator door and eat it straight from the mixing bowl as soon as I get home from work.

You can eat it as an appetizer or as part of a full meal with an assortment of other appetizer-like foods. These might include Greek olives, imported tuna fish packed in olive oil, baba ganoush (page 203), hummus (page 202), menfarake (page 112), hunks of feta cheese, cucumber and yogurt salad (page 63). Add some pita bread and a white wine such as Italian Pinot Grigio, California Savignon Blanc, or simply a decent jug wine from California, and you have an irresistible summer meal.

Since tabouleh is such an adjustable dish, I wouldn't take the following recipe too seriously. I like it green and lemony. You, however, may want to add more or less of everything.

1 cup bulgur wheat (mediu.n or
    coarse)
Water
1 cup fine-chopped scallions
    (including part of green)
1-1/2 to 2 cups fine-chopped
    parsley
1/2 cup fine-chopped fresh
    mint leaves or 4 tablespoons
    dried mint

1 teaspoon salt
1/4 teaspoon fresh-grounc black
    pepper (or more to taste)
1/2 cup olive oil
1/4 cup lemon juice (2 lemons)
    (or more to taste)
2 tomatoes, diced (optional)

1. In a large mixing bowl, cover the bulgur wheat with cold water by about 1 inch. Let soak 45 minutes to an hour, until wheat is tender, but not mushy. Remove it to a colander or strainer.

2. Dry out the mixing bowl, then place the scallions in it and, with the bottom of a water tumbler, press the scallions to extract some of their juices.

3. Drain the wheat. Take the bulgur by handfuls and squeeze out any excess moisture.

4. Add the parlsey, mint, salt, pepper, olive oil, and lemon juice to the scallions. If using dried mint, let the mixture stand about 10 minutes before continuing.

5. Add the cracked wheat and toss gently but thoroughly. Taste for salt, pepper and lemon juice, add more if necessary. Garnish salad with chopped tomatoes, if desired. *Makes about 6 appetizer or side-dish servings.*

TUNA AND CAPONATA (ITALIAN EGGPLANT APPETIZER)

My friend Nancy Arkin of Washington, D.C., once threw this salad together for a quick lunch and it virtually changed my life. I dieted on it for several months, never felt overly deprived, and lost a lot of weight. I still use it for quickie meals, but it is also a good appetizer.

The quality of canned caponata varies drastically from brand to brand, so do try to find a good one, although even the lesser brands are made edible by this doctoring. If you have any cold homemade ratatouille (see page 158), the French cousin of Italian caponata, use it instead and you will certainly have a superior salad.

1 7-ounce can tuna, preferably
   light chunk
1 6- to 8-ounce can caponata
   (Italian eggplant appetizer)

1 small red onion, chopped fine
1 small green pepper, seeded and
   diced fine

Combine all the ingredients and mix gently but well. *Makes 2 servings as a luncheon or light supper dish.* Serve with a green salad, tomatoes, and crusty bread.

NORTH AFRICAN CHOPPED SALAD

This little salad was first introduced to me as an accompaniment to a dish of lentils and rice flavored with cumin and fried onions, a typical Syrian or Egyptian peasant dish. I've since realized, however, that North Africans use this salad all the time and with many foods, including the ubiquitous sandwich in pita, flat pouched bread. You might consider serving it as an accompaniment to broiled lamb, baked kibbeh (see page 216), hamburgers or lamb burgers, menfarake (see page 112), or lamb in yogurt (see page 156). Also use it to top souvlaki sandwiches (page 171) or place it on a platter of assorted appetizers.

2 medium ripe tomatoes
1 medium cucumber, peeled if
   skin is waxed
3 scallions
3 or 4 fresh mint leaves, chopped
   (do not use dried mint)

2 to 3 tablespoons olive oil
1-1/2 teaspoons lemon juice
Salt and pepper to taste

1. Cut the tomatoes and cucumber into 1/4-inch cubes.

2. Cut the scallions into thin slices, using about half the green part.

3. In a bowl, combine the vegetables and remaining ingredients. Refrigerate until serving time.

CUCUMBER AND YOGURT SALAD

You can use any number of shredded vegetables with a dressing of yogurt, garlic, and herbs, but cucumber is particularly refreshing.

2 medium cucumbers, peeled and seeded
1 teaspoon salt

1 cup yogurt
1/2 to 1 clove garlic, mashed
1/2 teaspoon dried mint or dill

1. If you have a food processor, use it to shred the cucumbers. Otherwise use the shredding side of a four-sided grater and grate the cucumbers directly into a colander placed in the sink.

2. Toss the cucumbers with salt and let stand for 30 minutes. Press the cucumbers down to drain off excess water.

3. In a mixing bowl, combine the cucumbers with the rest of the ingredients and mix well. Serve immediately or chill until serving time. *Makes 2 generous servings.*

CARLO'S MUSHROOM SALAD

Carlo Caruso made this salad as an appetizer for all the local politicians and doctors who frequented the eatery on Long Island where he used to be the headwaiter. Now he owns one of the most highly regarded Italian restaurants in Montreal, Papagallo Urbino, and he has opened another stylish place in North Miami, Florida. He still serves this as an appetizer at both his restaurants, but I think it's even better with a plate of cold roasted meat or chicken.

1/2 teaspoon salt
2 to 3 teaspoons lemon juice
6 tablespoons olive oil
1 or 2 cloves garlic, crushed with
    the side of a knife

Fresh-ground black pepper to
    taste
3 tablespoons fine-chopped
    parsley
1 pound mushrooms, sliced

1. In a small bowl, dissolve the salt in the lemon juice. With a fork, beat in the olive oil, then stir in the garlic, pepper, and parsley. Let stand until ready to dress salad. The longer the dressing stands, the more garlic flavor it will have.

2. Just before serving, slice mushrooms and place in a salad bowl or mixing bowl. Beat dressing with a fork, taste, and add more lemon juice, salt, or pepper, if desired. Pour over mushrooms and toss. *Makes 4 servings.*

Note: If it is necessary to slice mushrooms ahead of time, sprinkle them with a little lemon juice and reduce the amount of juice in the dressing accordingly.

SLICED TOMATOES AND MOZZARELLA CHEESE

When tomatoes are at their peak you will be tempted to make this dish often if you can also get fresh mozzarella still dripping with whey. Fresh mozzarella is available in big cities in Italian markets, but not in many other places. I don't think you should bother with this if all that's available to you is the rubbery kind of mozzarella that's sold in supermarkets. Commercial mozzarella is good only for cooking, and often only marginally acceptable for that. If fresh mozzarella is unavailable, try eating your tomatoes with just anchovies, olive oil, and black pepper—also addictive. Crusty bread is a necessity either way, and whether you serve this as a first course or meal in itself.

3 to 4 ripe tomatoes
1 pound mozzarella cheese
Anchovies (optional)

Olive oil
Fresh-ground black pepper

1. Slice the tomatoes about 1/4 inch thick. Slice the cheese about 1/4 inch thick. Arrange the slices on a serving plate, alternating and slightly overlapping the tomatoes and cheese.

2. If using anchovies, arrange the whole fillets over every few slices or in a crisscross pattern over the tomatoes and cheese.

3. Drizzle with olive oil and grind on black pepper to taste. Salt is usually not necessary unless the cheese is unsalted. *Serves 2 as a main course or 4 as an appetizer.*

Variation: Garnish the plate with black or Greek olives and a sprinkling of fine-chopped parsley or basil.

COLD NOODLES WITH HOT SESAME SAUCE AND RAW VEGETABLES

This is a good salad to serve in a make-your-own salad bar format. Place the cold oil-dressed noodles in a large serving bowl and place the dressing and various vegetables in separate small bowls around it. Set out chopsticks and plates. If you want to serve a second sauce, so there's a choice, prepare the dressing that goes on the cucumber salad, page 63.

1 pound thin egg noodles spaghetti, or linguine
2 tablespoons vegetable oil
7 tablespoons Chinese sesame paste or 100% natural peanut butter
2/3 cup warm water
6 tablespoons soy sauce
2 tablespoons rice, cider or white vinegar
2 tablespoons sesame oil or corn oil

1 tablespoon cayenne pepper
1 tablespoon sugar
1 teaspoon salt
1 tablespoon fine-chopped garlic
3 to 4 whole scallions, chopped fine
1 bunch watercress, washed and thoroughly dried
2 large carrots
2 cups raw bean sprouts
1 whole scallion, chopped fine

1. Boil the noodles until just tender. Drain in a colander, then rinse under cold water, tossing the noodles with your hands, until thoroughly cooled. Drain very well, shaking out as much water as possible.

2. In a large serving bowl, toss noodles with the oil. (This is most easily and amusingly done by lifting and tossing them with two chopsticks.) Set aside. (May be made as much as a day ahead, but noodles are best if eaten within several hours.)

3. If the sesame paste or peanut butter has separated, drive a chopstick repeatedly into it until you can mix the oil in sufficiently to stir, although it needn't be perfectly smooth at this point.

4. In a small mixing bowl, with a fork, beat the sesame paste or peanut butter with the water until fairly smooth. Add the soy sauce, vinegar, sesame or corn oil, cayenne pepper, sugar, and salt. Beat until smooth. Add the garlic and scallions, stir well, and let stand at least 30 minutes or until ready to serve. (May be made several days ahead. Allow to return to room temperature before serving.)

5. With a large knife, chop the watercress coarse. Shred the carrots on the coarse side of a four-sided grater or in a food processor. Arrange the watercress, carrots, and bean sprouts on a platter or in separate bowls. Garnish noodles with a little chopped scallion and serve separately from vegetables and sauce. Everyone mixes the salad to taste. *Makes 4 servings as the sole main course.*

LONG ISLAND STRAWBERRY SOUP

Strawberries are a major crop in eastern Suffolk County and this soup is a major attraction at Silvers in Southampton, an establishment that is a crazy and chaotic mixture of tobacco shop, newspaper-magazine stand and restaurant. Cook-owner Danny Wellin told Barbara Rader of *Newsday* that this recipe is one that his family brought with them from the Crimea. To me it seems uncannily typical of Southampton.

1 quart fresh hulled and rinsed
    strawberries
1 pint heavy cream
2 ounces Grand Marnier liqueur

1/4 teaspoon almond extract or
    1 tablespoon Amaretto liqueur
4 ounces fine-ground hazelnuts

1. In a blender or food processor, combine the strawberries, heavy cream, Grand Marnier, and almond extract or Amaretto. Process until pureed.

2. Pour into serving bowls and sprinkle with hazelnuts. *Makes 4 servings.*

CARPACCIO

I have eaten carpaccio many tines in Italy and several times in the United States, but every time I've eaten it it has been different. Carpaccio is always made with raw beef, but I've been served it with raw mushrooms alone and with mushrooms and shavings of Parmesan cheese. It was onced passed around at a cocktail party on pieces of warm toast slathered with pesto. And I've had it dressed with just oil and lemon juice and with a vinegar dressing that included anchovies, garlic, and capers.

The most memorable carpaccio I had, however, was also the simplest. It was served at Badia da Coltibuono in Gaiole. The thin mean slices were vitellone (young beef), they were covered only with thin slices of woodsy mushrooms, and each diner made the dressing to his own taste using cruets of green Tuscan olive oil, freshly picked lemons, and pepper from a mill. If you can, get fruity olive oil and flavorful mushrooms (I think the mushrooms everyone avoids, the timeworn-looking ones with their gills showing, have beautiful flavor); it is worth making this way. However, I've served this to friends who disagree. They like the pizazz of anchovies, garlic, and capers. If you think you would, make a vinaigrette dressing instead of serving oil and lemon and simply add whatever you want to taste.

You will have to ask your butcher to cooperate with you in order to make carpaccio, since the meat should be sliced on an electric meat slicer. Tell him to partially freeze the meat and cut it as thin as he can without tearing it too much. The only other alternative is buy a shell steak, slice it about 1/4-inch thick and pound it out thin with a meat mallet or pounder.

Warning: Once, convinced that if a little serving of carpaccio is good, a large serving would be heaven, I served about six ounces of raw meat to each person. It wasn't a disaster, but it was a lesson: Raw food is much richer and harder to digest than cooked food and should be consumed in modest quantities.

Olive oil
1 pound beef fillet, sliced as thin
as possible (or use shell steak
and pound it thin)
Coarse salt
Fresh-ground black pepper

3 lemons
3/4 to 1 pound mushrooms,
sliced as thin as possible (you
might use a swivel-bladed
vegetable peeler)

1. Generously oil individual plates or one large platter and arrange the meat, preferably only slightly overlapping the slices.

2. Season with salt and pepper. Drizzle about 2 tablespoons oil and the juice of half a lemon over the meat.

3. Arrange the sliced mushrooms in the center of each plate or on the platter. Serve a half-lemon, either seeded or wrapped in cheese-cloth, with each serving. Place a cruet of olive oil, coarse salt, and a pepper mill on the table for guests to dress the meat and mushrooms themselves. *Makes 4 to 6 servings as a second course—perhaps after a bean soup—6 to 8 servings as a first course.*

Variation: To taste, add one or several of these to a basic three parts oil to one part vinegar dressing and use instead of just lemon and oil: mustard, mashed garlic or anchovies, chopped capers, chives, and/or shallots. For slivers of Parmesan cheese, shave a solid piece of cheese with a swivel-bladed vegetable peeler.

SEVICHE

Seviche is Peruvian, and as far as I know it is the only Peruvian dish to become an international classic. Although the fish is not cooked conventionally by heat, the citrus juice does marinate the raw fish to a "cooked" texture. Therefore, don't bother to warn squeamish guests about the fish's true nature. Serve seviche as part of a cold buffet, as a formal first course, as a party appetizer, or, with baked sweet potatoes, corn on the cob, and butter to spread on them, as a main course.

2 pounds fresh filleted fish or 1
  pound fish plus 1 pound shelled
  and deveined shrimp and/or sea
  scallops
3/4 teaspoon salt
2 medium onions, sliced thin
1 cup lime and/or lemon juice

1 large clove garlic, chopped fine
3 to 4 fresh hot peppers (or to
  taste), seeded and neatly diced
1 small ear corn, boiled for 3
  minutes
2 medium ripe tomatoes, seeded
  and neatly diced

1. With a sharp knife, cut the fish into 1/4-inch strips. Cut shrimp on the bias to get thin slices as large as possible. Slice scallops thin.

2. In a large ceramic, glass, or stainless steel vessel, combine all the ingredients except the corn and tomatoes. Stir to coat all the fish with juice.

3. Refrigerate 8 hours or overnight, stirring once or twice.

4. Just before serving, strip the kernels off the ear of corn with a sharp knife. Stir corn kernels and diced tomatoes into the fish mixture. Taste for seasoning. The hotness of peppers dissipates somewhat and you may want to add more or serve some diced peppers on the side. As an appetizer, serve with tortilla chips. If serving as main course with corn on the cob, eliminate the corn kernels. *Makes about 8 appetizer servings or 4 main course servings.*

One-Pot Dinners

A French politician representing a somewhat backward district in Africa was some time ago found to have been eaten by his constituents. The journalist who discovered this used the phrase: "Je crois qu'il a passé par la casserole" (I think he ended up in a casserole). Clearly the Africans knew what they were about. For making a delicious meal out of tough and intractable material, the casserole has no rival. . . .—Katharine Whitehorn, Cooking in a Bedsitter

It also has no rival for efficiency in a kitchen with limited space. In it you can prepare a satisfying and nearly complete meal even if all you have is a good hot plate on which to cook.

But I'd like to expand the notion of a casserole. The orthodox definition is a deep, covered dish, usually earthenware, in which a combination of foods are baked and usually served. (The word is sometimes applied to the food in the dish too.) Many dishes cooked in casseroles, however, are cooked either in the oven or on top of the stove, or are cooked exclusively on top of the stove. And sometimes you might refer to the dish in the pot as a stew or a fricassee or even a soup. And it isn't only an earthenware dish. It can be made of unclad cast iron, enameled cast iron, heavy aluminum, stainless steel, or copper.

I find the most practical casseroles are enameled cast iron. They heat fairly evenly on top of the stove or in the oven and they are attractive enough to be put on the table. Italian or French earthenware casseroles, unglazed on the bottom so they can be used on top of the stove, are also excellent cooking utensils. They are much less expensive than enameled cast iron and I think even more attractive on the table, but you must use them over moderate heat only. They are fragile. And most models do not come with covers, the usual cover being a dinner plate. For the recipes in this book you will need one small casserole of about three-quart capacity and one large one of at least five-quart capacity, although a larger size, seven or eight quarts, is more versatile. These casseroles are often called Dutch ovens, but not all so-called Dutch ovens can be used in the oven. Some contemporary designs have handles that are not heatproof and these are, therefore, less versatile—a distinct disadvantage when storage space is at a premium.

There is also another pot required for another kind of one-pot meal covered in this chapter, boiled dinners. For these you will need a large stock pot or at least an eight-quart casserole. This is a difficult pot to store in many small kitchens, but if you can find a spot for one or are willing to let it double as a wastebasket, a magazine and newspaper catchall, a log holder for near a fireplace, or some such thing, you will own a very useful pot. In it you can boil vegetables and meat together for a New England boiled dinner, prepare the Mexican boiled dish *pozzole,* or cook an elegant stuffed chicken with vegetables. It is the best pot for boiling pasta, offering plenty of room to cook it as it should be—in a generous amount of water. You can use it for large batches of soup, chili, or stew and, of course, for its intended purpose, making stock from meat bones or chicken. I even use mine for chilling several bottles of wine on ice for a party.

A pot for boiling does not necessarily have to be made of heavy metal that heats evenly, however. One of those old-fashioned white or blue enameled pots that are sold in housewares departments and hardware stores will do nicely, is quite inexpensive and much easier to handle than heavy enameled cast iron or thick aluminum. If you ever have to sauté or brown food in one of these light pots, though, watch closely and use only a moderate flame. The thin bottom of the pot makes scorching a likely possibility.

All the dishes in this chapter that require any accompaniment at all need merely a salad and bread. Followed by a cheese course or even just fruit, they make a substantial meal.

GARBURE

This is actually a soup, but it is so thick with beans, meat, and vegetables that it is virtually a stew, and all you need to complete the menu is wine, bread, a salad, and fresh fruit for dessert.

Garbure is a dish from the southwestern part of France, near Béarn but it is also loved in Bordeaux, and its traditional beverage accompaniment is red Bordeaux wine. The last drops of soup are usually mixed with the last drops of wine, perhaps a Côte de Fronsac, Côte de Bourg, or Côte Blaye appellation, and sipped directly from the bowl.

For a soup party menu, try a salad of watercress, endive, and leaf lettuce with chopped walnuts, oil (walnut oil if you can get it), and red-wine vinegar and a cheese tray between soup and dessert. Keep the wine flowing through the cheese course.

Although garbure can be reheated, I think it tastes best prepared no more than a few hours before being served. All the chopping preparation can be done a day ahead or over the course of a day and the vegetables placed in separate bowls and/or containers. Cover the potatoes with water and keep everything refrigerated. If you must prepare the soup a day ahead, remove the sausage and refrigerate both separately. Cut the sausage when you reheat the soup. If you have a large enough pot, this soup is easily doubled or tripled.

1/2 pound small white
  beans
1 pound Polish kielbasa
  sausage, smoked ham, or
  smoked pork shoulder
1 small head cabbage,
  shredded coarse
1-1/2 tablespoons chicken fat
  (optional)
1/2 pound string beans, cut
  into 1/2-inch pieces
1 white turnip, cut into
  1/2-inch cubes
1 onion, stuck with 4 whole
  cloves

2 pounds potatoes, peeled and
  cut into 1/2-inch-thick slices
1/2 teaspoon dried marjoram
  or 1/4 teaspoon dried
  oregano
1/2 teaspoon dried thyme
3 to 4 sprigs parsley
1/2 head garlic, still attached
  to core and unpeeled (about
  12 cloves)
1/2 pound chestnuts, roasted
  and peeled (optional)

1. A day ahead or the morning you plan to serve the garbure, bring 2 quarts of water to a rolling boil in a 3-quart saucepan. Add the beans and boil for 1 minute. Remove from heat and let stand 30 minutes. Return to heat and simmer for 30 minutes or until beans are just tender, but not fully done. Drain and reserve beans.

2. In your largest pot (it should be at least 6 quarts), bring 3 quarts of water to a rolling boil. Add the sausage or other meat and boil for 10 minutes.

3. Add remaining ingredients in the order listed and slowly enough that the water never stops boiling completely.

4. Lower heat so soup simmers slowly for about 1-1/2 hours.

5. Fish out the whole onion and the half head of garlic. Discard the onion. Squeeze the pulp out of the cloves of garlic and add to the soup.

6. Remove the sausage or other meat, cut into slices or cubes and return to the soup. Serve as soon as possible. *Makes 4 generous servings.*

CHICKEN AND ONION STEW

1 3-pound chicken, cut into serving pieces
1 teaspoon salt
1/4 teaspoon fresh-ground black pepper
3 tablespoons butter
1 tablespoon paprika
12 small yellow onions, peeled
2 tablespooons chopped celery leaves (if available)

1/2 pound mushrooms, sliced
1 tablespoon flour
3 ribs celery, cut into 1/2-inch diagonal slices
1-1/2 cups chicken broth
1/2 cup dry white wine
1/4 teaspoon dried thyme
1/2 cup sour cream

1. Pat chicken dry and sprinkle with salt and pepper. In a large Dutch oven or deep 12-inch skillet with cover, melt 2 tablespoons butter over medium heat. Sauté chicken gently, a few pieces at a time, until golden brown on all sides. Remove and set aside on a platter.

2. Lower heat, add a tablespoon more butter to pan, and stir in paprika. Add the whole onions and the celery leaves. Cook for 5 minutes, tossing onions frequently.

3. Add the mushrooms and continue to cook over low heat until mushroom liquid is exuded. Raise heat and allow mushroom liquid to evaporate. Blend in flour and cook another 3 minutes, stirring frequently.

4. Add celery, broth, wine, and thyme, stirring constantly. Return chicken to pan. Cover and simmer about 30 minutes or until chicken is done.

5. Just before serving, blend sour cream into pan sauce and heat through without boiling. Serve with a green salad and rye bread. *Makes 3 or 4 servings.*

OXTAIL STEW WITH CHESTNUTS

Do not be put off by the thought of oxtails. They offer some of the most flavorful meat on the animal and the bony tails make a fabulously rich sauce. Start dinner with the mushroom appetizer salad on page 63 and you won't need anything else but some hearty red wine to drink and plenty of crusty bread to clean up the mahogany sauce. For dessert, the Linzertorte on page 224 would be ideal — a comforting menu for the worst days of winter.

3 to 4 tablespoons vegetable oil
2 oxtails (about 4 pounds), disjointed (ask the butcher to do this)
1 cup flour
1 medium onion, chopped fine
2 cloves garlic, chopped fine
2 cups hearty red wine

3 cups beef broth (approximately)
1 teaspoon salt
1/4 teaspoon fresh-ground pepper
10 whole allspice berries or 1/4 teaspoon ground allspice
1 large bay leaf

2 medium turnips, peeled and
    cut into eighths
4 carrots, cut into 1-1/2-inch
    pieces

12 small white onions, peeled
    (see note)
16 chestnuts, roasted and
    peeled

1. In a large Dutch oven, heat the oil until very hot. Dry each piece of oxtail well in paper toweling. Place the flour in a brown paper bag. Shake a few pieces of oxtail at a time in the flour, shake off excess, then brown very well on all sides. (Dry and dredge the meat just before browning and brown only a few pieces at a time.) As each piece is browned, remove to a platter or bowl.

2. Pour off all but about 2 tablespoons of fat. Add onion and sauté 5 minutes or until tender. Add garlic and continue to sauté another minute.

3. Add wine and scrape up any browned bits sticking to bottom of pot. Bring to a simmer, then return oxtails to pot. Add beef broth to barely cover meat. Add salt, pepper, allspice, and bay leaf. Cover and place over very low heat or in a preheated 300° oven. Cook for about 2-1/2 hours, stirring occasionally. Liquid should reduce by about half. If it doesn't, remove pan to top of the stove over high heat. If too much evaporates, however, add a little more broth.

4. Taste and correct seasoning. Add the vegetables and chestnuts, stir, cover and return to oven or low heat for another hour. Skim off surface fat before serving. Serve with a green salad and crusty bread for mopping up the sauce. *Makes 4 generous servings.*

Note: To make peeling the onions easier, plunge them into boiling water for one minute, drain immediately, then let them cool enough to handle.

JAMBALAYA

In Louisiana kitchens jambalaya is not exactly a catchall, but is certainly considered adjustable to the occasion, immediate finances and the number of family members and friends that happen to drop by for dinner. In Creole country, the tomato and vegetable base for this paella-like dish might be prepared in the morning and, just before serving time, the appropriate amounts of sausage, crayfish, oysters, and shrimp (as much as was caught that day), rice, and possibly chicken would be added. The version here features spicy sausage, ham, and shrimp. Either a full white or light red wine is appropriate to go with it. To complete a festive menu, besides salad, serve boiled artichokes or asparagus with a dipping sauce for a first course (see pages 198-200) and the cheese-and-nut-filled crepes (page 244) with strawberries in two liqueurs or with hot fudge sauce for dessert.

6 tablespoons butter
2 medium onions, chopped
  fine
1 35-ounce can plum tomatoes
4 tablespoons tomato paste
3 large cloves garlic, chopped
  fine
2 large ribs celery, chopped
  fine
1 medium green pepper, diced
1/4 cup fine-chopped parsley

1/2 teaspoon dried thyme
1/4 teaspoon ground cloves
1/4 to 1/2 pound Creole
  chorice, Spanish chorizo or
  Italian pepperoni
2 to 3 cups cubed cooked
  ham (1 to 1-1/2 pounds)
3 cups boiling water
2 cups long grain rice
2 to 2-1/2 pounds shrimp,
  shelled and deveined

1. In a large casserole, melt the butter over medium heat and sauté onions until tender.

2. Add all the tomatoes and tomato paste. With a wooden spoon, break up the tomatoes, then add the garlic, celery, green pepper, parsley, thyme, and cloves. Stir well, then simmer 25 minutes. (May be prepared ahead to this point.)

3. Add the sausage and ham, return to simmer, and simmer another 5 minutes. Stir in the 3 cups boiling water and the rice. Cover and return to a simmer over high heat. Stir again, adjust heat to medium, re-cover, and simmer until rice is almost tender, about 12 minutes.

4. Stir in the shrimp and cook another 5 minutes or until shrimp are done, rice is tender and virtually all the liquid has been absorbed or evaporated. If, when adding the shrimp, there is still quite a bit of

liquid in the pot, cook shrimp uncovered. If mixture is already fairly dry, cook shrimp covered. Serve with a mixed salad. *Makes 6 to 8 servings.*

POLISH HUNTER'S STEW
(BIGOS)

A hearty dish for midwinter eating, this stew cries out for rye bread and beer, cucumbers with sour cream and chopped dill, pears for dessert. If you feel obliged to serve three formal courses, start out with caraway soup (see page 24, store-bought pickled herring in sour cream, mackerel in white wine (see page 215) or herring in mustard-dill sauce (see page 214). Finish with a Linzertorte (see page 222).

2 tablespoons lard or vegetable oil
2 cups sliced onions
2 pounds sauerkraut
2 tart apples, peeled, cored, and coarsely chopped
3/4 ounce dried Polish mushrooms
2 tablespoons tomato paste
1/2 cup water

1/2 teaspoon dried thyme
1 small bay leaf
1-1/2 tablespoon brown sugar
1/4 teaspoon fresh-ground black pepper
2 to 3 cups cubed cooked beef
1-1/2 pounds kielbasa (Polish sausage) cut into 1-1/2-inch hunks

1. In a large Dutch oven, heat the lard until very hot. Add the onions and sauté over medium-high heat until onions are well browned. Some of them should be rather dark, almost black. Be careful not to burn them totally, however.

2. Add the remaining ingredients, except meats. Stir well, cover, and simmer slowly for 2 hours.

3. Add the cut-up meats and continue to simmer another hour. Stew can be prepared entirely ahead and is even better when reheated. Serve with rye bread. No vegetable is necessary, but string beans are a good choice if you want one. *Makes 6 servings.*

SAUSAGE, POTATO, AND PEPPER BAKE

Everything is layered in a casserole and baked together for a simple but enticing blend of flavors and aromas. The potatoes, of course, absorb lots of the sausage fat and flavorful juices, but you'll still want some crusty bread to sop up what remains. This is a nice dish to throw together on a lazy Sunday for the family or a few close friends. Complete the menu with an appetizer of tuna and caponata salad (see page 61) and a green salad with or after the casserole. A California Zinfandel, Italian Barbera, or French Côte de Rhône wine would be just fine.

4 or 5 large potatoes, peeled
and sliced 1/4-inch thick
2 pounds sweet or hot Italian
sausage (mix them, if
desired)

4 large green and/or red
peppers, seeded and cut into
1/2-inch strips
2 tablespoons olive oil
Salt

1. Arrange the sliced potatoes on the bottom of a large casserole. Place the sausages, cut into separate links, over the potatoes. Arrange the peppers over the sausage. Drizzle the oil over the peppers and sprinkle lightly with salt.

2. Cover and place in a preheated 350° oven. If the ingredients slightly overflow the casserole, you can start the cooking with the casserole covered with foil. The ingredients will cook down enough at some point for you to be able to replace the foil with a cover. Bake for about 1 hour and 15 minutes and serve hot. *Makes 4 servings.*

FISH STEW WITH FENNEL

The base for this robust fish stew can be made ahead in a 3-quart saucepan. But because the clams take up so much room when they open, it will require at least an 8-quart pot to finish the stew. If you don't have one quite that large, substitute another less bulky seafood, such as scallops, or a second variety of fin fish. Or simply steam the clams in a separate pot, then pour the clam juices into the stew before serving.

For a company meal, you might start with the hot salami loaf, *sformata di salami* (see page 192). Serve the stew with an Italian white wine such as Frascati or Verdicchio, or, for a change with fish, a chilled red one, a young and light Chianti (not a *reserva*). Put the stew in bowls over boiled rice or, as a conceit, over small seashell macaroni. Salad can go with the stew or after it. In summer you could serve melon balls with rum and brown sugar for dessert.

1/4 cup olive oil	Fresh-ground pepper to taste
2 medium onions, chopped fine	2 pounds firm fish fillets, such as whiting
3 large cloves garlic, chopped fine	1 pound medium or large shrimp, shelled and deveined
1 cup dry white vermouth	18 littleneck or cherrystone clams, scrubbed well
1 teaspoon fennel seed	
1 35-ounce can tomatoes with tomato paste	1/3 cup fine-chopped fresh parsley
2 cups bottled clam juice	4 cups cooked rice (approximately)
3 cups water	
1 teaspoon salt	

1. In a 3-quart saucepan or a large pot in which you will cook the whole stew, heat oil and sauté onions over medium heat until golden. Add garlic and sauté a minute or two longer.

2. Add the vermouth and stir over high heat for a minute. Add the fennel seed and cook a few seconds more.

3. Add the tomatoes and, with a wooden spoon, break them up into small chunks. Add the clam juice, water, salt and pepper. Simmer gently, uncovered, for 20 to 30 minutes or until most of the tomatoes have disintegrated. (May be prepared ahead to this point. If using a saucepan for the base, transfer it to large pot before adding fish and seafood. Bring to a simmer before continuing with recipe.)

4. Cut the fish fillets into serving pieces (2 to 3 pieces per fillet).

Add fish, shrimp, and clams to the stew base. Simmer, covered, for about 15 minutes or until clams open and fish is cooked. Stir in the chopped parsley.

5. To serve, place rice or macaroni in soup bowls or deep plates, then ladle stew over the rice. Serve immediately. *Makes about 6 servings.*

A CROATIAN MIXED MEAT AND VEGETABLE CASSEROLE

This is solid peasant food, and a dinner featuring it doesn't even need a salad. It's a good buffet dish because all the ingredients are cut into pieces that are manageable with fork alone and it reheats very well.

1/4 pound bacon, chopped fine
1 pound each of boneless beef, lamb, and pork, each cut into 1-1/2-inch cubes
2 medium onions, sliced
2 cloves garlic, chopped fine
2 medium carrots, sliced
2 ribs celery, sliced
1 parsnip root, sliced (optional)
1-1/2 pounds small new potatoes
1 cup canned plum tomatoes

1 large green pepper, seeded and cut into strips
1/4 pound green beans, cut into 1-inch pieces
1/2 10-ounce box frozen peas
1/2 small head cabbage, shredded
2 tablespoons white vinegar
2 cups water
4 cups dry white wine
1-1/2 teaspoons salt
1/2 teaspoon fresh-ground black pepper

1. In a large casserole, cook the bacon over medium-low heat until some of the fat is rendered. Remove bacon and set aside in a bowl.

2. Increase heat to medium-high and brown the cubed meats on all sides in the bacon fat. As meat is done, transfer it to the bowl.

3. Add the onions and garlic to the fat in the casserole and cook over medium heat until onions are tender.

4. Layer some meat over the onions, then continue layering with other vegetables. Pour on the vinegar, water, and wine. Season with salt and pepper. Shake the casserole from side to side a few times to mingle the liquids.

5. Cover and place in a preheated 300° oven for about 4 hours or until meat is tender, or cook very slowly on top of the stove. Serve directly from the casserole. *Makes at least 8 servings.*

SOUTH AFRICAN STYLE LAMB AND BLACK-EYED PEAS

This is a highly seasoned dish for winter family meals, and you'll want a green salad after it to refresh your palate. For dessert try a cooling sherbet or melon balls with rum and brown sugar (see page 243), possibly over vanilla ice cream.

3 tablespoons vegetable oil
3 medium onions, sliced thin
2 pounds lamb shoulder, cut into 1-inch cubes
Salt and fresh-ground black pepper
4 tablespoons lemon juice (2 lemons)

1 teaspoon curry powder
4 canned green chilies, seeded chopped
2 large cloves garlic, crushed
1/4 teaspoon sugar
2 1-pound cans black-eyed peas

1. In a large casserole, heat the oil and sauté onions over medium heat until golden.

2. Add lamb, season with salt and pepper, and continue to cook, tossing frequently, until meat loses its raw color.

3. Add the lemon juice, stir well, cover, and place in a preheated 350° oven for about 30 minutes.

4. Add the curry, chopped chili peppers, garlic, and sugar. Mix well, cover, and return to oven for another 30 minutes or until meat is almost tender.

5. Add beans, mix well, cover and return to oven until meat is nearly falling off the bones. *Makes about 6 servings.*

PROVENÇAL STEW

This stew has been passed among my friends and acquaintances for so many years that I am, quite frankly, bored with it by now. But I do remember when it seemed most appealing to me and with all this popularity I'm sure it must be just as good as it seemed the first time I ate it. It is also one of the simplest recipes imaginable. You don't even have to brown the meat, and I know this counts for a good deal with many people.

2 ounces (about 4 slices)
   bacon or salt pork, chopped
   coarse
5 medium onions, sliced thick
5 cloves garlic, chopped coarse
3 pounds beef chuck, cut
   into 1-1/2-inch cubes
Peel of 1/2 large orange, cut
   into 1/4-inch strips
1/4 cup olive oil

2 whole cloves
1 large bay leaf
1 teaspoon dried thyme
1 tablespoon salt
1/2 teaspoon fresh-ground
   black pepper
3 tablespoons tomato paste
1 fifth full-bodied dry red
   wine

1. In a large casserole, combine the bacon, onions, garlic, beef chuck, and orange peel. Add the olive oil, cloves, bay leaf, thyme, salt and pepper.

2. In a small bowl or cup, dissolve the tomato paste in about a half-cup of wine. Pour into casserole, then add enough wine to barely cover all the ingredients.

3. Cover and place in a 300° oven for 3-1/2 to 4 hours or until meat is tender. Or cook with cover slightly askew on top of the stove, over the lowest possible heat, for 3 to 3-1/2 hours. When the casserole is

three-quarters cooked, if the sauce is ending up too thin and not concentrated enough, uncover the pot more. Serve in bowls over rice or macaroni. *Makes about 8 servings.*

CHOLENT

One of the great bean casseroles of the world, the eastern European cholent is made in an infinite number of ways, all of which could kill. This is heavy cooking at its heaviest. And as if it didn't have enough starch already with barley, beans, and potatoes, some people bury a piece of kishke (stuffed derma) in it as well.

You won't need anything after this, except a nap. And this is, in fact, what the Jews who made this dish probably did. Prepared as a Sabbath meal, the cholent would be brought to the local bakery oven, which was still hot from the baking of Sabbath challah, and cooked slowly until the end of Sabbath, when it was picked up on the way home from synagogue.

1 *quart water*	1 *13-3/4-ounce can beef broth*
1-1/2 *cups small dry lima beans*	2 *heaping teaspoons salt*
3 *tablespoons chicken fat or*	1/2 *teaspoon fresh-ground*
vegetable oil	*black pepper*
2-1/2 *to 3 pounds boneless*	1 *tablespoon paprika*
chuck or brisket	1/2 *teaspoon ground ginger*
2 *cups coarse-chopped*	4 *large cloves garlic,*
onions	*chopped fine or crushed*
1/2 *cup barley*	1 *large bay leaf*
2 *pounds potatoes, peeled*	

1. In a 2- to 3-quart saucepan, bring a quart of water to a rolling boil. Pour in the beans, return to a boil and boil for 2 minutes. Remove from heat and let stand 1 hour.

2. Meanwhile, in a large casserole, heat the vegetable oil over high heat. Pat the meat dry with paper toweling and brown well on all sides.

3. Lower heat to medium, add the onions, and sauté until tender. Pour the lima beans and their water over into the casserole. Sprinkle the barley around the meat, then arrange the potatoes around the meat.

4. In a cup, stir into some of the broth, the salt, pepper, paprika, ginger, and garlic. Pour over the meat, then add remaining broth and enough water to just cover everything. Shake the pot from side to side a few times to mingle the liquids. Bury the bay leaf in the pot.

5. Cook the cholent, covered, on top of the stove, on the lowest possible heat. The liquid should barely simmer. Do not stir. Cook for at least 5 hours, longer if possible. Or, cook the cholent, covered, in the oven, at 200° to 250° for 10 to 12 hours. When first done, the ingredients in the cholent will still have some shape, but many people like the cholent reheated, then reheated again, until it is mushy and almost a hash. *Makes about 8 servings.*

VEAL STEW WITH TARRAGON

A lovely dish for informal company, especially in spring when you can start with asparagus or artichokes and finish with a strawberry dessert. California dry Chenin blanc is a good wine choice.

*2 pounds stew veal (1 to
  1-1/2-inch cubes)*
*3 large carrots, scraped and
  cut into 1-inch pieces*
*2 medium onions, chopped
  very fine*
1 teaspoon salt
1/8 teaspoon cayenne pepper
2 tablespoons flour

2 tablespoons water
*3/4 pound mushrooms, sliced
  thin*
1/2 teaspoon dried tarragon
2 egg yolks
*1/2 cup heavy cream or sour
  cream*
1 teaspoon lemon juice

1. In a 3- to 5-quart casserole combine the veal, carrots, and onions. Add enough water to just cover. Season with salt and cayenne and bring to a simmer. Partially cover and simmer gently for 45 minutes

to 1-1/2 hours or until meat is almost tender. (Timing depends on quality of meat.)

2. In a cup, dissolve the flour in 2 tablespoons cold water then stir into the veal stew. Stir until liquid thickens slightly. Add the mushrooms and tarragon and simmer uncovered for another 15 minutes.

3. In a small cup or bowl, beat together the egg yolks and cream. Add to the stew and, stirring constantly, heat through without boiling. Stir in lemon juice. Serve in bowls with boiled new potatoes. *Makes 4 to 6 servings.*

TAMALE PIE

This is one of those kinds of recipes that still fill women's magazines. It is easy, economical, and good plain eating. It is nothing more than a sort of chili with corn bread topping. In fact, instead of the following meat combination you might use a favorite chili recipe and simply top it with the corn batter outlined below.

1 medium onion, chopped fine
1 medium green pepper, chopped fine
1 pound lean ground beef
1/4 teaspoon fresh-ground black pepper
1/2 teaspoon salt
1 tablespoon chili powder
1 16-ounce can plum tomatoes with their juice
1/3 to 1/2 cup sliced pimento-stuffed olives

For topping:
1/2 cup sifted all-purpose flour
1/2 cup cornmeal
1 teaspoon baking powder
1 tablespoon sugar
1/4 teaspoon salt
1/3 cup milk
1 egg
2 tablespoons melted butter or vegetable oil

1. In a 3-quart casserole, combine the onion, green pepper, and ground beef. Place over medium-high heat and cook until meat has lost its raw color. Stir and break up mixture constantly and carefully because it will more than half-fill the pot at this point.

2. Stir in the pepper, salt, and chili powder, then add the tomatoes, breaking them up with a wooden spoon. Simmer about 20 minutes. Skim off visible fat. Stir in olives. (May be prepared ahead to this point. Set aside and, if cold from refrigeration, remove hardened fat and reheat to a steady simmer before adding the topping.)

3. In a mixing bowl, combine the flour, cornmeal, baking powder, sugar, and salt. Mix well.

4. In a small bowl or cup, beat together the milk and egg, then stir into the dry ingredients. Stir in the melted butter or oil, then pour the batter over the simmering meat mixture.

5. Cover and cook at a slow but steady simmer for 15 minutes, then uncover and cook 15 minutes more. *Makes 4 servings.*

COUNTRY CAPTAIN

This is an unusual curry dish which Georgians claim for their own. Its history is not clear. But "country captain" was a British name for a captain of the Sepoys, East Indians who served under them as soldiers and may, or may not, have introduced this Anglo-Indian treatment to the Southern gentry. I prefer a sweet wine or beer with curry.

8 slices bacon
2 2-1/2- to 3-pound chickens,
　cut into pieces
1 medium to large onion,
　chopped
2 medium green peppers,
　diced
1-1/2 tablespoons curry
　powder
1 tablespoon flour
2 cloves garlic, mashed
1/2 teaspoon thyme

1 28-ounce can plum
　tomatoes
1/2 cup raisins or currants
Salt and pepper to taste
For garnishes:
1 bunch scallions, chopped
　(including green part)
1 cup unsalted peanuts
1 cup shredded coconut
　(preferably unsweetened)
Reserved bacon, crumbled

1. In a large casserole or deep 12-inch skillet, cook the bacon over medium heat until some of the fat has rendered. Raise heat and cook bacon until crisp. Remove bacon and set aside on absorbent paper.

2. Brown the chicken in the bacon fat a few pieces at a time, drying the chicken well before adding to the fat. As chicken is done, remove to a plate.

3. Pour off all but 2 to 3 tablespoons of fat. Add the onion, green peppers, and curry powder. Sauté over medium heat until onion is tender, scraping up any browned bits from the chicken.

4. Add remaining ingredients (except garnishes) and, with a wooden spoon, break up the tomatoes. Simmer for 5 minutes, then add salt and pepper to taste, seasoning well. Add the chicken, turn in the sauce, cover and simmer for about 35 minutes or until done. Serve over boiled rice or lentils. Serve garnishes on the side in separate bowls. *Makes 6 to 8 servings.*

UNSTUFFED CABBAGE

I, like many people, love stuffed cabbage but don't like stuffing it. Besides, it takes a considerable amount of counter space to organize the effort. I find this recipe using sauerkraut and meatballs is a good compromise. It has a similar flavor without any of the work. And you can make it for a small group and be assured that the leftovers will taste even better when you attack them in solitary. Serve with rye bread or boiled potatoes and beer. A soothing cheesecake is good for dessert.

2 pounds sauerkraut
(preferably fresh or jarred,
not canned)
1 25-ounce can tomato puree
1/2 cup dark brown sugar
2 cups beef broth or bouillon
1/2 to 3/4 cup seeded raisins
or pitted prunes

Salt and fresh-ground black
pepper
2-1/2 pounds ground beef
1/2 cup raw rice
Salt and fresh-ground black
pepper

1. Drain the sauerkraut and if it is very sour, place in a strainer or colander and rinse it quickly under cold water.

2. In a large casserole, combine the sauerkraut, tomato puree, sugar, broth or bouillon, and raisins. Stir well and bring to a simmer over medium heat. Simmer gently, uncovered, for about 10 minutes. Then taste and add salt and pepper as desired.

3. While sauce is cooking, combine the meat and rice in a large bowl and season to taste with salt and pepper. Form meatballs the size of golf balls (the mixture should yield about 24) and drop into the sauce. Cover and simmer gently, stirring occasionally, for about 1-1/2 hours. *Makes 6 to 8 servings.*

NEW ENGLAND BOILED DINNER

4 to 5 pounds corned beef
  brisket
10 whole cloves
7 bay leaves
12 small yellow onions, peeled
8 medium potatoes, peeled
  and cut in half

8 carrots, cut in half
1 large head cabbage, cut in
  sixths or eighths
8 beets (optional)

1. Place the brisket in a large kettle or stock pot. Pour on cold water to cover by a few inches, add the cloves and bay leaves. Bring to a boil, skim off scum, then reduce heat and simmer gently for about 1-1/2 hours. (May be prepared ahead to this point. Remove meat from broth if holding more than an hour. Vegetables should be cooked just before serving.)

2. Add the onions and simmer 30 minutes longer. Add potatoes and carrots and simmer 15 minutes longer. Add cabbage and simmer 10 to 15 minutes more or until the meat and vegetables are tender, but not overcooked.

3. Meanwhile, if serving optional beets, cook them separately, covered with water, in a saucepan until tender, 45 to 60 minutes, depending on size of beets.

4. To serve, slice meat and arrange in the center of a serving platter. Surround with vegetables and serve with mustard and/or horseradish or a horseradish sauce. Serve beer or hard or sweet cider. *Makes about 8 servings.*

MARIE BIANCO'S BELGIAN WATERZOOI OF FISH

Mrs. Bianco, who writes the "Feedback" food question-and-answer column in *Newsday*, is always searching for quickly prepared dishes to serve her large family. This is one of her finds.

4 tablespoons butter	1 bay leaf
2 carrots, sliced	1/2 teaspoon thyme
2 medium leeks (white parts only), sliced	1/4 teaspoon ground cloves
1 small onion, sliced	2 tablespoons fine-chopped parsley
2 pounds fish fillets (cod, haddock, perch)	Salt and fresh-ground black pepper to taste
1 quart water	1 lemon, sliced
2 cups dry white wine	Fine-chopped parsley

1. In a large casserole, melt butter and sauté carrots, leeks, and onion over medium heat until soft but not browned.

2. Cut the fish into large chunks and place over the vegetables. Add water, wine, bay leaf, thyme, cloves, parsley, salt, and pepper.

3. Bring to a simmer over high heat, adjust heat and simmer gently for 20 minutes. After 15 minutes add the lemon slices. Remove bay leaf. Serve in soup bowls with boiled new potatoes and a sprinkling of parsley. *Makes 4 to 6 servings.*

POZOLE

This recipe was contributed to *The New York Times* by a reader a number of years ago. It was offered to show how a very complicated, albeit totally authentic, Mexican recipe could be simplified and still be quite delicious. It is a make-your-own sort of dish where everyone gets to add to taste the various garnishes and flavorings that go into the basic boiled pork and hominy base. This makes for a great deal of amusing confusion at the table as well as less work for the cook in the kitchen. (Whole hominy is often available at stores that cater to Latin Americans.)

1 4- to 5-pound fresh ham or pork loin (preferably one of the fattier ends)	4 medium avocados, diced into one-inch chunks
2 cloves garlic, crushed	1 large Spanish onion, diced
2 tablespoons coarse salt	2 5-ounce packages corn chips
4 quarts water	2 bags fried bacon rind
4 14-ounce cans whole hominy	1/4 cup crushed red chili pepper
4 large limes, cut into eighths	1/4 cup oregano

1. In a large pot, combine the pork, garlic, salt, and water. Bring to a boil over high heat, then adjust heat and simmer until meat is tender. Timing depends on quality of meat.

2. Remove the pork and shred the meat, discarding the fat. Place the meat in a bowl, cover with broth from the cooking, and set aside until ready to serve. Cool the remaining broth and skim off the fat. (May be prepared ahead to this point.)

3. Bring the broth to a boil and add the hominy with half the liquid from the cans. Discard remaining liquid. Simmer 20 minutes.

4. All remaining ingredients, except avocado, can be arranged in small serving dishes in advance. It is best to cut avocado soon before serving because it discolors rapidly. To retard the discoloration, place the avocado pits in the bowls with the diced pulp.

5. In a soup bowl, serve some meat, hominy and broth to each person. Allow everyone to add remaining ingredients to taste, warning them to add things such as lime, chili, and oregano slowly until they achieve their desired result. *Makes 6 to 8 servings.*

BILLY'S ADOBO

This is the Philippine national dish as prepared by a friend from Missouri. Just dump everything into one pot and you can say you've cooked. Billy does.

4 chicken breast halves,
 skinned
4 inch-thick center-cut pork
 chops
15 cloves garlic, chopped
 coarse
1 cup soy sauce
3/4 cup white distilled
 vinegar

2 cups water
2 tablespoons sugar
6 large bay leaves
1 tablespoon fresh-ground
 black pepper
Boiled rice

1. In a large casserole, combine all the ingredients except rice. There should be just enough liquid to cover the chicken and meat. Add more soy sauce, vinegar, and water if there isn't.

2. Shake the pot to mix the liquids. Bring to a boil, uncovered, over high heat, then adjust heat and cook gently for about 1 hour. Serve in bowls over boiled rice. *Makes 4 servings.*

MADAME BRUNO PRATS' STUFFED HEN BORDELAISE

The Prats are an important Bordeaux wine family and their best known wine is Clos D'Estournel, a second-growth from the commune of Saint-Estèphe. As a wine to drink with this dish, however, Madame Prats suggests the less complex and expensive wine from the family's Château Falfas in the Côte de Bourg. If you don't have a food processor to chop the veal, prosciutto, and liver together, purchase ground veal and chop the livers and ham fine with a chopping knife on a board.

3/4 pound veal, ground if
  necessary
1/4 pound prosciutto or
  boiled ham
3 chicken livers
1 medium onion, chopped
  fine
2 shallots or scallions, chopped
  fine
1/4 cup fine-chopped parsley
1 egg
2 tablespoons milk

1/2 teaspoon dried thyme
Dash nutmeg
Salt and fresh-ground pepper
  to taste
1 4-pound roasting chicken
3 carrots, cut into 1-inch pieces
3 ribs celery, cut into 1-inch
  pieces
6 small onions, peeled
Cold water
1 small head cabbage, cut
  into eighths

1. In a food processor, chop the veal, prosciutto, and livers together until fairly fine. Empty into a large mixing bowl. Or, chop the prosciutto and livers fine and combine with ground veal in a mixing bowl.

2. Add the onion, shallots, parsley, egg, milk, thyme, nutmeg, salt, and pepper. Knead together very well.

3. Stuff the chicken with the veal mixture and sew or skewer the chicken closed.

4. Place the chicken in a large pot and cut in the carrots and celery. Add the onions. Cover by one inch with cold water and bring to a boil over high heat. Cover, adjust heat and simmer for about 1-1/2 hours or until chicken is tender. Add cabbage for the last half hour or cook separately.

5. Madame Prats serves the chicken garnished with cornichons (sour gherkins), with the carrots, celery and onions pureed together and the cabbage in wedges. A food processor makes the vegetable puree an easy matter, but the dish is also fine with the vegetables served as is. If you haven't cooked the cabbage in it, the broth makes a fine soup, a first course to which you can add some pasta.

Skillet Cooking

Skillet, frying pan, chicken fryer, sauteuse, or sauté pan—whatever you call it, it's one of the most useful pieces of kitchen equipment you own, especially if you are forced by the limits of your appliances always to cook on top of the stove.

My most useful skillet is a deep, twelve-inch, heavy aluminum French sauté pan with a tight fitting cover that also fits my stockpot. It is very large for my small stove, intruding on the cooking space around it, but heats up extremely well anyway, and I think it pays to have large pieces of equipment even in a small kitchen. At any rate, don't purchase a sauté pan smaller then ten inches in diameter. Almost every recipe in this chapter can be made in a ten- or twelve-inch skillet. Either size is large enough to cook two chickens at once, but not so large that one can't be done successfully. Both are too large for sautéing small amounts of food but are very practical for sautéing or pan-broiling veal, liver, chops, and steaks even when there are as few as two to feed. Mine has a handle with a hole at the end so I store it on a hook on the back of the broom closet door. The cover gets stashed on top of the stockpot, which has its own shelf and is large enough to keep odds and ends in. (In small kitchens everything that can has something inside it.) An eight-inch skillet will also get used often, if only for frying eggs and omelets. To make crepes you'll need a six-inch skillet as well. The very large, deep skillet or sauté pan must have a tight-fitting cover, but a large heat-resistent dinner plate will often suffice for smaller pans.

Good cookware makes good cooking easier and quality pots and pans last a lifetime, if not several. But the most expensive is not necessarily the best or most practical. Prohibitively expensive heavy copper pans are a dream to fry and sauté in, but inexpensive old-fashioned cast-iron pans are also wonderful cooking utensils. Both require some care—copper needs to be shined regularly; cast iron must be dried immediately after washing to avoid rust. Stainless steel, between the two in price, offers easy maintenance but should have heavy reinforced bottoms for better heat conduction. Don't bother with stainless pans with thin copper cladding on the bottom. The copper is too thin to be anything but cosmetic. One can purchase heavy copper pots lined with stainless steel, but these are priced like works of art, which they are, in a way. Heavy aluminum is an excellent skillet material and not expensive, but it can discolor and give a metalic bite to acidic foods, such as tomatoes or sauces with wine, when they are left in the pan too long. Remove these foods from the pan as soon as they are finished cooking.

A number of the dishes in this chapter—skillet steak pizzaiola, Mediterranean beef skillet dinner, chicken chasseur, and chicken with spicy fruit sauce—are practically meals in themselves. Add a salad, bread, or other appropriate starch and fresh fruit for dessert for a very respectable informal menu. There are also a few Chinese recipes, which are traditionally cooked in a wok but can just as easily be done in a large skillet. There are three veal recipes, all quickly prepared, to serve with a salad or steamed vegetable on workdays and, with a few well-chosen accompaniments, for more formal occasions.

Omelets are a natural for this chapter, but instead of recipes for French-style omelets I've outlined the method for making Italian frittate. They are easier to do well and, because they are delicious hot or at room temperature, more useful. Steak au poivre for two, a Middle Eastern scrambled egg and ground meat dish for a meal in a hurry, a bread baked in a skillet for the ovenless and a from-scratch version of the Armenian rice and vermicelli pilaf that the ads say is a "San Francisco treat" finish the chapter.

CHICKEN SAUTÉS

The basic French chicken sauté cooks just in the chicken's natural juices, a bit of butter or oil, and a few seasonings, while the classic fricassee contains a considerable amount of liquid and is what most people would call a stew. The following four recipes really fall somewhere between the two.

In all of them the chicken is first browned in a fat, then cooked with a relatively small amount of seasoned liquid, which becomes the sauce. The same basic techniques are used in all the recipes. Their differences in taste depend on the fat, seasoning, and liquid used.

Although only one pot is needed to prepare a chicken sauté—a large, deep skillet with a cover—you will also need a large platter on which to put the chicken after it is brown and while you scrape up the browned bits from the skillet and stir in the liquid and seasonings. To reserve your counter space for more necessary functions, like chopping a vegetable or putting down a spoon, place this platter right on top of the stove near the pan you're working in or keep it in the off or very low oven. I use an oven-proof oval platter that was very inexpensive at a restaurant supply house.

CHICKEN DIJON

2 tablespoons butter
2 tablespoons vegetable oil
1 2-1/2- to 3-pound chicken,
    quartered or cut into pieces
1 small onion, chopped fine

1 clove garlic, chopped fine
1-1/2 cups chicken broth
2 tablespoons Dijon mustard
1/2 teaspoon dried tarragon

1. In a 10- to 12-inch skillet, heat the butter and oil together over medium-high heat and brown the chicken well, a few pieces at a time, on all sides. Make sure to dry each piece of chicken well before placing in skillet. Remove to a platter as the chicken gets done.

2. Pour off all but about 2 tablespoons of fat. Add the onion and garlic and sauté about 1 minute.

3. Add the broth and scrape up any brown bits from the skillet.

4. Blend in the mustard and tarragon. Return chicken to the skillet, cover and simmer slowly, turning the chicken twice, for about 35 minutes.

5. Transfer chicken to a warm platter. Skim excess fat off sauce and raise heat under skillet. Boil sauce briskly, stirring constantly, until sauce is thick and syrupy. Spoon sauce over chicken and serve immediately. *Makes 2 to 3 servings.*

CHICKEN CHASSEUR

3 tablespoons vegetable oil
2 tablespoons butter
2 2-1/2- to 3-pound chickens, cut into pieces
3/4 pound mushrooms, sliced thin
2 tablespoons fine-chopped shallot or scallion (white part only)
2 tablespoons flour
3/4 cup dry vermouth
3/4 cup beef broth or bouillon
1 1-pound can imported plum tomatoes, drained and chopped

1 large clove garlic, mashed or chopped fine
1/2 teaspoon dried tarragon
1 tablespoon fine-chopped chives or scallion tops
1/4 teaspoon dried thyme
Salt and fresh-ground black pepper to taste
2 to 3 tablespoons fine-chopped parsley

1. In a 10- to 12-inch skillet, heat that oil and butter together. Over medium-high heat, brown the chicken pieces well on all sides. Make sure to dry each piece of chicken well just before adding to the skillet. Do not crowd skillet. As chicken is browned, remove to a platter.

2. When all the chicken is browned, in the same skillet, sauté the mushrooms over low heat until their moisture begins to exude. Increase heat to medium and sauté until almost all the liquid has evaporated.

3. Add the chopped shallots or scallions and cook until all the liquid is gone. Blend in flour and cook about 3 minutes longer.

4. Add the vermouth and bouillon, stirring constantly. Bring to a simmer, then add the tomatoes, garlic, tarragon, chives, and thyme. Season to taste and stir well.

5. Arrange the chicken back in the skillet, cover, and lower heat so liquid barely simmers. Cook 25 to 30 minutes or until chicken is done.

6. Place the chicken on a platter. If the sauce is not concentrated enough, boil it briskly, uncovered, until reduced sufficiently. Stir in parsley, then pour sauce over chicken and serve immediately. *Makes 4 to 6 servings.*

LEMON CHICKEN

2 tablespoons butter	1/4 cup lemon juice
2 tablespoons olive oil	1/2 teaspoon dried oregano
1 3-pound chicken, cut into serving pieces	1 teaspoon salt
1 small onion, chopped fine	1/4 teaspoon fresh-ground black pepper
2 cloves garlic, chopped fine	2 tablespoons fine-chopped parsley
1/3 cup water	

1. In an 10- to 12-inch skillet, heat butter and oil together over medium-high heat. Dry the chicken pieces in paper towels, then, a few pieces at a time, brown well on all sides. Remove chicken to a bowl or plate as it is done.

2. Add the onion and garlic to the skillet and sauté until onion is tender, scraping up any browned bits from the bottom of the skillet.

3. Add the water, lemon juice, and seasonings. Stir well, then return the chicken to the skillet, turning the pieces in the pan liquid.

4. Arrange chicken skin-side-down, cover, and simmer 15 minutes.

5. Turn chicken and continue to cook until done, about another 10 minutes. If necessary, add more water by tablespoonfuls.

6. Remove chicken to a serving platter and spoon pan juices over it. *Makes 2 to 3 servings*

CHICKEN WITH SPICY FRUIT SAUCE

1 2-1/2- to 3-pound chicken, cut
    into serving pieces
Salt and fresh-ground black
    pepper
3 tablespoons vegetable oil
2 to 3 tablespoons slivered
    blanched almonds
1/2 cup seeded raisins

1 cup drained crushed pineapple
    packed in natural juice
1/4 teaspoon cinnamon
1/8 teaspoon ground cloves
1/8 teaspoon cayenne pepper
2 cups orange juice
1 tablespoon cornstarch dissolved
    in 3 tablespoon water

1. Dry chicken in paper towels, then sprinkle liberally with salt and pepper.

2. In a 10- to 12-inch skillet, heat oil and brown chicken, a few pieces at a time, over medium-high heat. As chicken is done, remove to a plate.

3. Reduce heat to medium, add all the remaining ingredients, except dissolved cornstarch, and scrape up any browned bits on the bottom of the skillet. Return chicken to skillet, cover and simmer gently 25 to 30 minutes or until chicken is done. Arrange chicken on a serving platter.

4. Add dissolved cornstarch to the sauce in the skillet and cook over medium heat until thickened. Correct seasoning if necessary. Coat the chicken with some of the sauce and serve remaining sauce separately. *Makes 2 to 3 servings.* Serve with boiled rice.

CHICKEN IN DILL SAUCE

1 4-pound roasting chicken, cut
    into serving pieces
4 tablespoons butter
3 bunches scallions, sliced thin
    (white and green parts)
1/4 cup chopped fresh dill or 2
    tablespoons dried dill weed)

1-1/2 cups water
Salt to taste
3 eggs, separated
3 tablespoons lemon juice
    (1-1/2 lemons)

1. In a 10- to 12-inch skillet, over medium heat, sauté chicken in half the butter until golden, but not brown, on all sides. Remove to a platter.

2. Add the remaining butter. Then add the scallions and dill. Continue cooking over medium heat until scallions are tender.

3. Add the water. Bring to a simmer. Season with salt and pepper. Return chicken to skillet, then cover and simmer gently until chicken is tender, about an hour. (May be prepared ahead to this point. Reheat through before continuing with recipe.)

4. Just before chicken is done or heated through, in a large mixing bowl with an electric hand mixer, beat the egg whites until stiff.

5. When done, arrange chicken on a warm serving platter and keep warm.

6. Add yolks and lemon juice to the beaten whites and continue beating, gradually adding the hot juices from the skillet. Pour sauce over chicken and serve immediately. *Makes 4 to 5 servings.* Serve with roasted potatoes or boiled rice.

CHICKEN AND ASPARAGUS IN BLACK BEAN SAUCE

Although a wok is efficient and amusing to cook in, it is an absolutely unnecessary pan to own. Any dish that can be stir-fried in a wok can also be prepared in a conventional skillet.

Cubes of chicken and short lengths of asparagus cut diagonally so they will cook quickly are combined here with a penetrating but not overpowering black bean sauce. The essential fermented black beans need to be purchased at a store that carries Chinese foods, but all the other ingredients are readily available at the supermarket. The beans, once you obtain them, can be kept virtually indefinitely in a plastic container or jar.

As in most Chinese stir-fry cooking, the cutting, chopping, and assembling of ingredients can be done well before you plan to cook.

Place the various groups of prepared ingredients in small bowls or plastic containers ready to be added to the pan. You can store them in the refrigerator just to keep them out of the way, but before you put a light under the skillet, arrange the containers conveniently close to the stove or place all the ingredients in separate piles on a platter that can be put on one of the inactive burners. Actual cooking time is no more than five or six minutes.

*1 tablespoon fermented black
    beans
1 tablespoon hot water
2 cloves garlic, mashed
1 tablespoon soy sauce
1 pound fresh asparagus
2 boneless chicken breast halves*

*1 tablespoon cornstarch
2 tablespoons cold water
1-1/2 tablespoons vegetable oil
1/2 teaspoon salt
1-1/2 tablespoons vegetable oil
1/2 cup chicken broth
1/2 teaspoon sugar*

1. In a small bowl or cup, using a fork, mash together the black beans and hot water. Stir in mashed garlic and soy sauce. Set aside.

2. Cut asparagus spears diagonally into 1-inch pieces, discarding the tough white ends. Set aside.

3. Cut chicken breast halves into 1-inch squares. Set aside.

4. In a cup, dissolve the cornstarch in the 2 tablespoons cold water. Set aside.

5. In a large skillet or wok, heat 1-1/2 tablespoons oil over high heat. Add the chicken pieces and 1/2 teaspoon salt. Stir-fry until chicken loses its pink color. Remove with a slotted spoon and set aside on a plate.

6. Add the remaining 1-1/2 tablespoons oil and stir-fry the black bean mixture for about 5 seconds. Add the asparagus and stir-fry 1 minute.

7. Stir in the chicken broth and sugar. As soon as liquid begins to boil, reduce heat to medium.

8. Return chicken to the skillet, cover and simmer gently for 2 minutes.

9. Blend in dissolved cornstarch and stir until sauce thickens. Serve immediately. *Makes 2 servings with just rice, more with other dishes.*

CHINESE PEPPER STEAK WITH TOMATOES

Again, a skillet will do just as good a job as a wok. Overcooking is the biggest flaw with dishes like this. The vegetables should keep their shape and remain slightly crunchy. Actual cooking time should be no more than 5 minutes.

3 small firm, ripe tomatoes, each cut into 6 to 8 wedges
2 medium green peppers, seeded and cut into 1/2-inch wide strips
2 small onions, sliced thin
1 teaspoon sugar
4 teaspoons soy sauce
1/2 teaspoon fresh-ground pepper
1/2 cup beef bouillon or broth

4 tablespoons dry sherry
1-1/2 tablespoons cornstarch
1/4 cup cold water
2 cloves garlic, crushed
1 teaspoon fine-minced fresh ginger root
2 whole scallions, chopped fine
4 tablespoons vegetable oil
1 pound flank steak or round steak, cut into strips 1/8-inch thick and 2 inches long

1. In a small bowl, combine the tomatoes, peppers, and onions. Set aside.

2. In a cup, combine the sugar, soy sauce, pepper, bouillon, and sherry. Set aside.

3. In another cup, dissolve the cornstarch in the water. Set aside.

4. On a saucer, combine the garlic, ginger, and scallions.

5. In a large skillet or wok, heat the oil until very hot. Add the garlic mixture and stir-fry a few seconds. Add the sliced meat and stir-fry 1 minute.

6. Add the vegetable mixture and stir-fry another minute.

7. Add the bouillon mixture, mix well, then give the cornstarch and water a quick stir with a fork and add to skillet. Stirring constantly, cook until thickened. Serve with boiled rice. *Makes about 4 servings.*

EXPLODE-IN-THE-MOUTH CHICKEN

For a party this is an excellent finger-food to serve with beer or cocktails, but not wine, except perhaps a dry or medium-dry sherry.

1 3-pound chicken, cut into
  bite-size pieces
1 tablespoon soy sauce
  (preferably dark soy)
1 egg white
1-1/2 cups vegetable oil
4 dried chili peppers, cut in half,
  seeds removed
1-1/2 teaspoons fine-chopped
  garlic

1 tablespoon fine-chopped fresh
  ginger
2 tablespoons soy sauce
  (preferably dark soy)
1 tablespoon white vinegar
1 teaspoon cornstarch
3 tablespoons water
1/2 teaspoon sugar
Pinch salt

1. In a large bowl, mix the chicken pieces, 1 tablespoon soy sauce, and egg white.

2. In a large skillet or wok, heat the oil over high heat. Add chicken and fry, stirring occasionally, until lightly browned, about 15 minutes. With a slotted spoon, remove the chicken and set aside in the large bowl.

3. Pour off almost all the oil, leaving just enough to coat the skillet or wok. Add chili peppers and fry until they begin to turn black.

4. Meanwhile, in a small bowl or cup, mix 2 tablespoons soy sauce, vinegar, cornstarch, water, sugar, and salt together.

5. When the peppers are done, add the garlic and ginger and stir-fry about 15 seconds.

6. Return the chicken to the skillet and immediately add the liquid mixture. Allow chicken to sizzle a few seconds with the sauce, stirring constantly. Serve immediately with plain boiled rice. *Serves 2 as a main course.*

STEAK AU POIVRE FOR TWO

Shell steak, also called Kansas City or New York strip steak, is often the cut one gets when ordering this dish in a restaurant. You might also use a porterhouse or T-bone steak — in which case you will need only one large one for two people — or filet mignon, which is famous for its tenderness but has a rather bland flavor that could use a fiery treatment like this.

*2 teaspoons (or more) black
  peppercorns*
Salt to taste
*2 10- to 12-ounce shell steaks or
  other steaks*
1 tablespoon vegetable oil

1 tablespoon butter
2 tablespoons cognac
1 tablespoon butter
1/4 cup heavy cream
Salt to taste

1. Place peppercorns in the corner of a clean kitchen towel and bang with a heavy object to crush them coarse.

2. Season the steaks with pepper on both sides, pressing the pepper into the steaks with the heel of your hand. Salt to taste. Let stand at least an hour.

3. In a large skillet, heat the oil and butter together over high heat. Before the butter burns, add the steaks and cook from 3 to 7 minutes per side, depending on thickness of steak and desired degree of doneness.

4. Place the steak on a warm platter. Pour off the fat in the pan.

5. To the hot skillet, add the cognac, fresh tablespoon of butter, and the heavy cream, in that order. Quickly scrape up any browned bits from the bottom of the pan, mix well, check for salt and serve over steaks immediately.

SKILLET STEAK PIZZAIOLA

This dish has little relation to genuine Italian cooking, but it never was intended to. It was developed in response to, and more or less in imitation of, the packaged skillet dinners that were such a craze a few years ago. Tasting considerably better than any packaged skillet meal, however, it is a worthy dish for an informal dinner. With enough sauce to pour over macaroni, a mixed salad or a buttered vegetable is all else you need to serve with it. And since I said this wasn't truly Italian, be altogether un-Italian and serve the macaroni with the meat, instead of before.

2 pounds boneless chuck steak	1 teaspoon salt
2 tablespoons olive oil	1/4 teaspoon fresh-ground
1 medium onion, chopped fine	black pepper
1 1-pound can imported plum	1 small green pepper, chopped
tomatoes	fine
1/4 teaspoon dried oregano	6 to 8 ounces mozzarella cheese,
1/4 teaspoon dried basil	shredded
2 cloves garlic, mashed	1 pound macaroni

1. Steak should be about 1/2-inch thick and cut into pieces about 4 by 3 inches. If steak is too thick, pound it out a little with the bottom of a heavy water tumbler or a meat mallet.

2. In a 10- to 12-inch skillet, heat the oil and brown the steak well on both sides over medium-high heat. Lower heat to medium, add the onion, and sauté a few minutes longer to wilt the onion.

3. Add the tomatoes and their juice and break them up with a wooden spoon. Add the oregano, basil, garlic, salt, and black pepper. Stir to mix, cover, and simmer slowly 40 to 60 minutes, stirring once or twice.

4. When meat is almost tender, add green pepper, stir, re-cover, and continue to simmer until meat is tender, probably another 10 to 15 minutes. (May be prepared ahead to this point and when cooled to

room temperature, refrigerated for a day or two. Reheat slowly but thoroughly before continuing with recipe.)

5. Bring a large pot of water to a boil for the macaroni and begin to cook macaroni about 15 minutes before serving.

6. When meat is fork tender, ladle off at least half of the sauce. Reserve this for the macaroni. Sprinkle shredded cheese over the meat, cover skillet and place over low heat 3 to 4 minutes or until cheese melts. Meanwhile, drain the cooked macaroni and toss with sauce. *Makes 4 to 6 servings.*

MEDITERRANEAN BEEF SKILLET DINNER

This is strictly a quick, homey meal with which you will want a salad, bread and red wine.

2 tablespoons olive oil
1 medium onion, chopped
1-1/2 pounds lean ground beef
1 1-pound can plum tomatoes,
  drained
2 cloves garlic, chopped fine or
  crushed
1/2 teaspoon dried thyme
1/8 teaspoon ground cinnamon

1 eggplant (about 1 pound),
  peeled and cut into 1/2-inch
  cubes
1 cup (about 4 ounces) shredded
  Switzerland Swiss cheese
1/4 cup grated Parmesan or
  Romano cheese

1. In a 10- to 12-inch skillet, heat the oil and sauté the onion over medium heat until tender.

2. Add the meat, raise heat to high, and break up the meat with a wooden spoon. Cook until it has lost its raw color.

3. Add the tomatoes and break them up with the spoon. Add the garlic, thyme, and cinnamon. Mix well. Add the eggplant, cover and let simmer, stirring occasionally, about 15 minutes or until eggplant is tender.

4. Sprinkle on the shredded Swiss cheese, then grated cheese. Cover and continue to simmer gently another minute or until cheese has melted. Serve immediately. *Makes 2 to 3 servings.*

A Trio of Veal Sautés

The next three dishes, two of which are on almost every Italian restaurant menu, all follow a similar preparation pattern — the veal is cooked quickly in a skillet and removed to a plate, the sauce is made in the same skillet, then the veal returns to the skillet just long enough to be turned and flavored with the glazelike sauce. All are easy and quick to prepare, although they must be done at the very last moment. Ask the butcher to pound the veal for you.

VEAL PICCATA

2 tablespoons butter	Flour
1 tablespoon vegetable oil	Juice of 1/2 lemon
1 pound veal cutlets (cut from the leg), pounded thin	2 tablespoons dry white wine
	1 tablespoon fine-chopped parsley
Salt and fresh-ground black pepper	Lemon wedges

1. In a 10- to 12-inch skillet, heat the butter and oil together over medium heat.

2. As the fats heat, begin preparing the veal. Dry each piece with paper towels, then sprinkle lightly with salt and pepper. Dredge in flour, poured onto a dinner plate, then cook quickly over high heat. The cutlets should not need more than about 30 seconds per side. Do not crowd the pan. As the cutlets are done, remove to a plate.

3. When all the cutlets have been cooked. immediately add the lemon juice and white wine to the skillet. Cook a few seconds, stirring constantly, then return cutlets to skillet with any juices that have collected in the plate. Turn the veal in the glazelike sauce, then arrange the pieces on a plate and serve sprinkled with parsley and garnished with lemon wedges. *Makes 3 or 4 servings.*

Variation: To make so-called veal Francese, dip the veal in beaten egg, then flour. Instead of butter and oil, cook the veal in enough oil to cover the bottom of the skillet by 1/4 inch. When the veal has been cooked, pour off all oil and add 1 tablespoon butter before adding the lemon juice and wine.

VEAL MARSALA

Use only imported dry Marsala. The dish is not worth making with domestic or sweet marsala.

3 tablespoons olive oil
1/2 pound mushrooms, sliced thin
2 ounces prosciutto or boiled ham, chopped
1 pound veal cutlets (cut from the leg), pounded thin

Salt and fresh-ground black pepper
Flour
1/2 cup dry imported Marsala wine
Fine-chopped parsley (optional)

1. In a 10- to 12-inch skillet, heat the oil and sauté mushrooms and ham together over medium heat until mushrooms are tender but not browned.

2. Meanwhile, season the veal cutlets lightly with salt and pepper. Dredge in flour, which has been poured onto a dinner plate, and shake off excess.

3. When mushrooms are done, remove with a slotted spoon and place on a plate.

4. Increase heat slightly and sauté veal cutlets about 30 seconds on each side. Do not crowd pan. As cutlets are done remove them to the same plate.

5. Add the Marsala and cook over high heat until reduced by half. Return the mushrooms, ham, and veal cutlets to the skillet. Turn the cutlets in the sauce, then arrange on a platter, pour the sauce over them, and serve immediately. Sprinkle with parsley if desired. *Makes 3 or 4 servings.*

VEAL SCALOPPINE WITH ANCHOVIES, PINE NUTS, AND WHOLE GARLIC CLOVES

On each serving of veal, place a spoonful of nuts and a few whole cloves of garlic. Everybody squeezes the garlic out of its skin and eats it to taste with each bite of veal.

4 tablespoons butter	6 to 8 anchovy fillets, chopped
2 tablespoons of vegetable oil	fine
1 bay leaf	1 pound veal cutlets (cut from the
8 to 12 whole cloves garlic,	leg), pounded thin
unpeeled	1/4 cup dry white wine
2 heaping tablespoons of pine	1 tablespoon lemon juice
nuts (pignoli)	

1. In a 10- to 12-inch skillet, melt the butter and oil together. Add the bay leaf, garlic, and pine nuts and sauté over medium heat until pine nuts are beginning to get golden.

2. Lower heat, add the anchovies and continue to cook, stirring constantly, until the anchovies have disintegrated.

3. Raise the heat to medium-high and, in the same skillet, sauté the veal scallops for about 30 seconds on each side. As they are done, remove to a serving platter.

4. Add the white wine and lemon juice. Simmer, stirring constantly, until reduced slightly. Discard the bay leaf, return the cutlets to the skillet just long enough to turn them in the sauce, then arrange them on a plate. Pour sauce with pine nuts and whole garlic over the veal. Serve immediately. Whole garlic should be cut open by each diner and the soft tamed pulp eaten with bites of the meat. *Makes 3 or 4 servings.*

FRITTATE

Frittate (the singular is *frittata*) are the Italian equivalent of omelets, although they are not made like French omelets at all. Instead of the eggs being cooked into a thin pancake, then folded around a filling, as in French omelets, the eggs in a frittata are mixed and cooked with the added meat, vegetable or cheese. If the added ingredients need to be fried or sautéed, this can be done in the same skillet that the whole frittate will cook in. I find they are more versatile and less challenging than French omelets when space is limited. There is also a recipe on page 209 for a Spanish omelet that is made in the same way, although that one really requires two skillets for a first class result.

Frittate are traditionally served, either hot or at room temperature, as a light main course (perhaps after soup or pasta) or cut into wedges as an appetizer.

For an impressive vegetarian dish, stack a variety of vegetable frittate on top of each other and serve in wedges with a tomato or cheese sauce.

CHEESE FRITTATA

6 eggs
1/4 teaspoon salt
1/8 teaspoon fresh-ground black
  pepper

1/4 cup grated Parmesan cheese
1-1/2 tablespoons butter or olive
  oil (depending on preference)

1. In a mixing bowl, beat the eggs with the salt and pepper until light and well mixed. Beat in the cheese.

2. In a 6- to 8-inch skillet, heat the butter or oil over medium heat. When the fat is hot, give the eggs a final stir and pour into the pan. Immediately reduce heat as low as possible. Cook until the bottom is well set, usually about 6 minutes.

3. At this point, the top must be cooked in one of two ways. Slide the frittata out of the skillet onto a plate. Hold the skillet over the frittata and reverse the plate and the skillet so the frittata falls back in the skillet uncooked side down. Cook about a minute or until set.

4. Or, if you use a skillet with a heat-proof handle, such as an un-

coated cast-iron skillet, you may place the skillet under a broiler for about a minute or until the top of the frittata has set. *Makes 2 main-course servings.*

ASPARAGUS AND OTHER VEGETABLE FRITTATE

1/2 pound asparagus
1 tablespoon butter
1-1/2 tablespoons vegetable oil
Salt and fresh-ground pepper

7 eggs
1/4 teaspoon salt
2 tablespoons grated Parmesan
* cheese (optional)*

1. Cutting on a sharp diagonal to expose as much of the interior as possible, slice asparagus into 1-1/2-inch pieces.

2. In a 7- to 8-inch skillet, heat the butter and oil together over medium heat. Add the asparagus and season lightly with salt and pepper. Sauté, stirring and tossing frequently, for about 10 minutes or until asparagus are crisp-tender.

3. Meanwhile, beat the eggs with the salt and optional cheese until light and well mixed.

4. When the asparagus are done, pour the egg mixture into the pan and immediately lower heat. Cook as above. *Makes 2 main-course servings.*

Variations: Use the same method for similar amounts of any of the following vegetables: Rounds of zucchini and/or yellow summer squash, sliced onions or leeks (sauté until very tender), chopped broccoli, chopped spinach, thawed frozen, artichoke hearts, eggplant strips, diced green and/or red pepper or sliced mushrooms.

MENFARAKE

The name means "broken up" and menfarake is really nothing more than scrambled eggs with ground meat, Middle Eastern style—a pleasant change from European omelets, a quick supper for working people, and a good way for a single person to use up the leftovers from the amount of ground meat one is forced to buy at the supermarket.

1/4 pound lean ground beef	1/4 cup vegetable oil or com-
3 eggs	bination oil and butter
1/2 teaspoon salt	1/4 cup fine-chopped parsley
1/2 teaspoon ground allspice	

1. In a mixing bowl, combine the meat and eggs. Beat well as for scrambled eggs. Mixture should be fluffy. Beat in salt and allspice.

2. In a 6- to 8-inch skillet, heat oil (or oil and butter) over medium heat until very hot. Pour in egg mixture and cook, without stirring, until edges curl. Then, with a fork, stir until eggs cook into curds. Serve warm or at room temperature sprinkled with parsley. Serve with pita bread and North African chopped salad (see page 62), a mixed vegetable salad, or steamed zucchini. *Makes 1 or 2 servings.*

SYLVIA CARTER'S SKILLET BREAD

This is for the few people who may have no oven at all or for those whose ovens are so inaccurate that conventional baking is chancy at best. Sylvia can make a fine roast and perfect barbecued ribs in the tiny, primitive, and unregulatable oven in her kitchen-once-closet. She manages to produce wonderful cream biscuits too. She achieves these things, however, only because when she was a child she was taught how to make them on a wood-burning stove in Granger, Missouri. She offers this recipe for those whose backgrounds were not so fortunate.

2 cups sifted all-purpose flour	1 tablespoon butter
2-1/2 teaspoons baking powder	1 tablespoon peanut or corn oil
1 teaspoon salt	1-1/2 cups buttermilk
1/2 teaspoon baking soda	1 tablespoon butter

1. Into a mixing bowl, sift the dry ingredients together.

2. In a 10- to 12-inch skillet, melt the butter with the oil over medium heat.

3. While the butter and oil are heating, quickly stir the buttermilk into the dry ingredients, then spread the batter in the hot skillet.

4. Cover and cook over low heat for 12 to 15 minutes. Slide the bread out of the skillet onto a plate. Add another tablespoon butter to the skillet and return the bread, uncooked side down. Cover and cook another 12 to 15 minutes. Cut into wedges and serve hot or warm. *Makes 4 to 6 servings.*

ARMENIAN PILAF

This is a stove-top pilaf made in a skillet, better than any such packaged dish for serving with broiled meat or chicken.

1/2 cup butter	*2 cups chicken broth*
1/2 cup 1/4- to 1/2-inch long pieces of vermicelli or fine noodles	*1 clove garlic, chopped fine or crushed*
1 cup rice	*1 teaspoon salt*

1. In a 10- to 12-inch skillet, melt butter over medium heat. Add the vermicelli or noodles and sauté until lightly browned.

2. Add the rice, stir well to coat with butter and sauté 2 to 3 minutes, stirring constantly. Be careful not to burn the noodles.

3. Add the chicken broth, garlic, and salt. Cover and cook over very low heat for about 20 minutes or until broth has been absorbed and rice is tender. *Makes 4 servings.*

Broiling and Roasting

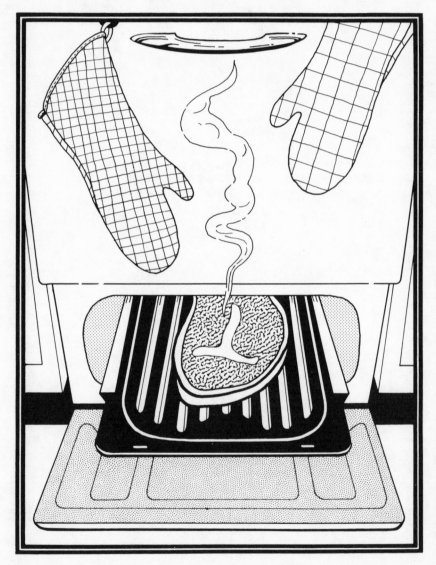

It is hard to argue with those who tout the convenience of broiling steaks, chops, and chicken for everyday meals or the ease with which standing ribs of beef can be roasted for company. In a small kitchen it is particularly useful to know how to roast and broil well, and throughout this book there are many menu suggestions that include roasted and broiled beef, lamb, chicken, and fish.

These cooking methods, however, require considerably more care and skill than most people suppose. Modern ovens and broilers, both gas and electric, are not exactly ideal appliances for such jobs. The minute-per-pound timetables that most everyone relies on are only a general guide at best. And the seeming simplicity of the methods encourages inattention to the task at hand.

A few practical hints for getting satisfactory results from an apartment oven and broiler follows, but long essays could be and have been written on roasting and broiling.

Meat should always be served on hot platters and dishes, so try to organize the top of the stove to fit a stack of dishes on one back burner where they will benefit from the heat generated by the oven.

Broiling

The most important thing to remember about broiling is that it requires intense heat. The broiler should be heated to the maximum of the appliance before you put the food in.

The distance between the food and the heat source is also important. For fish fillets and the average 1-inch to 1-1/2-inch steak or chop, the heat source should be rather close. In most broilers of my experience, this means the next to the closest groove, or about 3 inches from the heat.

For chicken, the heat needs to be further away or the skin will char before the inner flesh is cooked. The next rung down may be fine, but this will also depend on the plumpness of the chicken. If you can force the breasts to lie flatter by putting them on a steady surface and giving them one sharp bang with your hand, they will cook more evenly.

Fish steaks and fillets an inch thick or more, thick whole fish, shrimp, and scallops should be cooked 4 to 5 inches from the heat.

Pieces of meat that are less than 1 inch thick really need to be on the top groove of the broiler, but this usually puts them in the flame or on the coils rather than under them. You may have to remove the broiler insert to prevent this, in which case you might want to use a disposable aluminum broiling tray to keep the meat above the fat. Contrary to a lot of opinion, I don't find these particularly useful for broiling. They are flimsy and clumsy to handle and because the fat that cooks off the meat lies exposed to the heat they often cause flare-ups which give the meat a rancid burned-fat flavor. But in a case where you need to improvise to get the food as close to the heat as possible, if the food is well trimmed of fat, these aluminum pans are the answer.

Beef and lamb cuts do not need basting or preseasoning, although I do sometimes brush a steak with olive oil before putting it under the fire, and I like to marinate London broil round steaks and flank steaks occasionally for changes in flavor. Even if the meat has been marinated, however, the surface should be dry before you put it in the broiler.

Unless you buy it at a special ethnic market or from a farm where it has scratched around, chicken has very little flavor these days. So I advise always preseasoning it in some way, at least a rubdown with lemon and garlic or a coating of strong mustard.

Fish need to be basted with butter or oil or they'll dry out, but I don't think more than a few drops of liquid — white wine, lemon or lime juice—should be added for seasoning. More can always be added at the table.

Timing is, of course, all-important and impossible to give rules for. So much depends on the appliance, the thickness, shape, and quality of the meat and on taste. Touching the food is a good indicator of doneness, and experience will give you a feel for knowing just the right moment to stop cooking. A well-done steak will not give as much to the touch as a rare steak. A drumstick that shakes in its joint easily is more done (maybe overdone) than one that won't shake at all. Breast meat cooks more quickly than dark meat and when done will feel firm to a strong poke. You can also tell when chicken is done by sticking the point of a knife into a joint. If the juices run pink, the bird may not be fully cooked. The juices should run clear or yellow.

If you broil enough fish you'll eventually get a feel for its doneness too, but the fork method is ever reliable even if it does slightly ruin the appearance of the fish. Don't cook fish until it is in dry flakes, however. It is done when it is no longer gelatinous and the flakes are moist ones.

STEAK MARINADE

1 medium onion, cut in
  eighths
2 cloves garlic
1 teaspoon dried thyme
8 peppercorns

6 juniper berries or 2
  tablespoons gin
2 large strips lemon peel
1/4 cup olive oil
1 cup red-wine vinegar

In a blender or food processor, combine all the ingredients except half the vinegar. Process on high speed until all ingredients are thoroughly mixed and chopped. Add remaining vinegar and process until mixture is homogenous. Let meat marinate in refrigerator from 4 to 12 hours, turning several times. Broil to taste. *Makes about 1-1/2 cups—about enough to marinate a 4-6 pound steak London broil.*

LAMB OR BEEF MARINADE

1 cup hearty red wine
1/2 cup olive oil
3 cloves garlic, split
1 teaspoon dried marjoram
1 teaspoon dried thyme

1 bay leaf, crumbled
Few sprigs parsley
1/2 teaspoon fresh-ground
   black pepper

1. In a shallow glass pan, mix all the ingredients. Turn the meat in the marinade. Cover and refrigerate for up to 12 hours, turning occasionally. Or marinate about 3 hours at room temperature. *Makes about 1-1/2 cups, enough for at least 3 pounds of meat.*

BROILED LEMON CHICKEN

1/2 cup lemon juice
1/4 cup vegetable oil
1 large clove garlic, chopped
1/2 teaspoon celery salt
1/2 teaspoon salt
1/2 teaspoon fresh-ground
   black pepper

2 tablespoons grated onion
1/2 teaspoon dried thyme
1 2-1/2- to 3-pound chicken,
   cut in parts

In a mixing bowl, combine all the ingredients except chicken. Mix well. Place the chicken in a shallow glass, enameled, or stainless steel baking dish and pour the marinade over it. Let stand at room temperature for several hours or overnight in the refrigerator, turning the chicken several times. Broil as usual.

MADHUR JAFFREY'S TANDOORI CHICKEN

5 pounds chicken legs, thighs,
and breasts
Juice of 2 lemons
1 tablespoon kosher salt
1/2 cup plain yogurt
1 medium onion, chopped
coarse

1 clove garlic, chopped
coarse
One piece fresh ginger about
1-1/2 inches square
1/2 to 1 hot green chili, sliced
1 tablespoon garam masala
(see note)

1. Skin the chicken pieces. Cut each breast into four pieces. Detach legs from thighs if necessary. Cut deep diagonal slits in all the chicken pieces. (Slit the legs on two sides. The breasts and thighs can be slit only on the meaty side.)

2. Place the chicken on a baking sheet and sprinkle with the lemon juice and salt. Rub the lemon and salt into each piece of chicken. Set aside for 15 to 20 minutes.

3. Meanwhile, in a blender or food processor, puree the remaining ingredients together.

4. Spoon or brush this mixture on all the chicken, making sure it gets into all the slits. Place the chicken in a large stainless steel or non-metallic bowl. Cover with plastic and refrigerate at least 12 to 18 hours.

5. Arrange chicken on a baking sheet and preheat oven on broil. Place chicken in the top third of the oven and bake for 15 to 20 minutes or until the chicken is cooked through but not browned. Breasts may be done as soon as 10 minutes. *Makes 8 servings.*

Note: Garam masala is an Indian spice mix sold in specialty food shops.

SHANGHAI BARBECUED LAMB

This is a most impressive looking piece of meat and extraordinarily delicious too. For a buffet, serve it with cold noodles with hot sesame sauce and raw vegetables.

2 tablespoons soy sauce
2 tablespoons hoisin sauce
  (see note)
2 tablespoons dry sherry
1/2 teaspoon five-spice
  powder (see note)
1 tablespoon sugar
2 teaspoons fine-chopped
  fresh ginger root

2 scallions, chopped fine
  (white and green parts)
1 teaspoon sesame oil
3 pounds butterflied leg of
  lamb (about 4-3/4 pounds
  before boning)

1. In a small bowl or cup, mix all the ingredients except the lamb.

2. Place meat on a platter or in shallow baking dish and pour over the marinade mixture. With your hands, massage it into the meat, then let stand at room temperature about an hour. (Refrigerate if prepared more than a few hours ahead.)

3. Broil about 5 inches from the heat for about 12 to 15 minutes per side in an oven broiler or 15 to 20 minutes per side over a hibachi or other outdoor grill. Slice thin and serve. *Makes about 6 to 8 servings.*

Note: Hoisin sauce is a mahogany-colored condiment sauce made of soybeans seasoned with garlic, chili peppers, and sugar. It is available in cans and, if packed in a covered jar or plastic container and covered with a very thin layer of vegetable oil, will keep almost indefinitely in the refrigerator. It is delicious as a dipping sauce for roasted meat and poultry or instead of ketchup on a hamburger. If you cannot find Chinese hoisin sauce for this recipe, American ketchup, while not at all the same, can be substituted.

Five-spice powder, also called five-fragrance powder, is usually made from ground star anise and fennel seeds, cloves, cinnamon, and ginger, although the combination sometimes varies slightly. If you cannot find this spice already prepared, substitute 1/4 teaspoon ground fennel or anise seed with a pinch each of cinnamon, ginger and cloves. Or, use 1/4 teaspoon ground allspice with a pinch each of ginger and cinnamon.

Roasting

There are two reasons I suggest starting roasts at a high temperature, then reducing the heat to low to finish the cooking. The first is gastronomic, the second a reason only a small-kitchen dweller would have.

Gastronomically, I think meat is juicier when initially sealed or seared by high heat. And if you have a small roast—in the three-pound range—the outside will often not brown fully when the inside is cooked rare. High heat will brown it better. The practical small-kitchen reason is that the lower oven temperature for the bulk of the cooking time doesn't heat up the kitchen as much.

Start a roast in a 475° oven for about 25 minutes, then reduce it to 300° and cook the meat until done to taste. Roasting meat to exactly the right stage, however, can only be hit-or-miss without a meat thermometer stuck into the thickest part of the meat. You must also have a rack on which the meat can rest above the roasting pan and, of course, a roasting pan. The pan must be shallow—no higher than 2-1/2 inches—but that is its only requirement, and if you chose one carefully, it can be an extremely useful pan to own. (See page 222.)

Unfortunately, the temperature ranges given on most meat thermometers for the various stages of doneness are often too high. If you remove the meat when the thermometer indicates medium, it is more likely to be on the verge of well-done. Following then, on page 124, are the readings at which you should remove meats. The meat should always rest 10 to 15 minutes before carving, in which time it will cook a little more.

As in broiling, however, feel is often a better indicator of doneness than anything. When done, the meat should feel firm, neither stiff nor soft. Only experience can really teach you this.

For rare beef: 120°
For medium-rare beef: 125° to 130°
For medium beef: 135°
For well-done beef: 145° to 150°

For pink lamb: 145° to 150°
For well-done lamb: 155° to 165°

For pork: 165° to 175°

YORKSHIRE PUDDING

If you are roasting a large piece of beef, one of the best space-saving accompaniments is Yorkshire pudding, a giant popover made from the meat drippings and a simple batter in the same pan in which the meat roasted. While the roast recomposes itself before carving, the pudding bakes in the oven. You will, however, need to turn up the oven temperature before the pudding goes in the oven, which may in the summer create a little more heat than you can bear in the confines of your kitchen.

2 eggs	1 cup all-purpose flour
1 cup milk	1/2 teaspoon salt

1. Prepare the batter ahead of time. In a mixing bowl, beat the eggs and milk together with a wire whisk, then gradually beat in the flour and salt. Or, place all the ingredients in a blender or food processor and mix well.

2. When the roast is done, remove it and its rack. Place the roast on a platter to rest. Pour off all but about 4 tablespoons of beef dripping and place the pan back in the oven. Turn the oven up to 450°.

3. In 2 or 3 minutes, slide the roasting pan out of the oven and pour in the batter, to which you have given one last beating. Return to the oven immediately and bake for 8 minutes. Lower heat to 375° and bake another 20 minutes. Serve immediately with the roast. *Makes at least 4 servings.*

HERB-STUFFED LEG OF LAMB

If at all possible, prepare the stuffing before you purchase the meat and bring it with you to the butcher. He will undoubtedly have to bone the lamb to order and probably won't mind spreading the stuffing in the lamb for you so you won't have to tie the roast yourself. If this is out of the question, however, and you don't think you can manage tying the roast yourself, you can re-form the roast into a cylinder, tucking in odd ends, and secure the roll with a long skewer.

2 tablespoons olive oil
1 medium onion, chopped
  fine
1 cup fine-minced parsley
2 large cloves garlic, crushed
1 teaspoon dried thyme
1/2 teaspoon salt

1/4 teaspoon fresh-ground
  black pepper
5- to 6-pound boned and
  butterflied leg of lamb
  (about 8 pounds with bone),
  well trimmed of fat
Olive oil

1. In a medium skillet, heat the oil and sauté onion over medium heat for 2 minutes. Cover and continue cooking for 10 minutes.

2. Add herbs, salt, and pepper. Mix well and sauté another minute. Remove from heat and allow to cool.

3. Lay the meat out flat, boned side up, and spread the stuffing on it. Roll up and re-form into a cylindrical roast.

4. Rub oil into the surface of the meat and place in a preheated 500° oven for 20 minutes. Reduce heat to 375° and roast approximately 90 minutes longer. *Makes at least 10 servings, but is good cold.*

ROASTED KIDNEY

If you like kidneys, this is a nice recipe to make when there are just one or two people eating.

2 tablespoons vegetable oil
1 beef kidney with a layer of
   its fat intact
1 or 2 large potatoes, peeled
   and cut into large chunks

Salt and fresh-ground
   pepper

1. Grease a small baking dish and place the kidney in it. Place potatoes around it. Season with salt and pepper and place in a preheated 350° oven for about 45 minutes or until done to taste. Baste the kidney and potatoes several times with the fat that renders off the kidney *Makes 1 or 2 servings.*

Dinners for Two

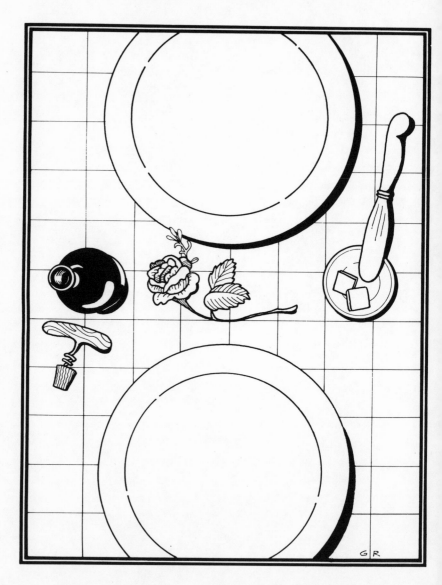

People, not food, make meals romantic. Yet I am very tempted to call a number of the following menus romantic dinners for two. Food IS sensual. And eating with someone dear to you CAN often be as erotic as sex itself.

Some of the menus below, however, are simply practical everyday meals. Others present foods – liver, tripe, sweetbreads – that have so few fans that you may have trouble finding more than one other person to eat them with. All the menus have been organized so that they won't overburden a small kitchen or a cook with limited experience, but any special problems they may present are discussed below.

A Rustic Italian Dinner for Intimate Friends

Salami, prosciutto, imported Provolone cheese
Bagna cauda
Crusty Italian bread
Strawberries in Zinfandel

To emphasize the sensual rusticity of this menu and to make it look like an opulent feast, don't put just a few thin slices of salami on a plate; put out a whole one and serve it on a board with a sharp knife for cutting it into servings. The same goes for the cheese. Buy a sizable hunk. In my house, salami and cheese never go to waste. The prosciutto, because you won't need and probably can't afford more than a quarter-pound, should be purchased in paper-thin slices and arranged neatly on a decorative plate. Wrap the bread in a large cloth napkin and

simply break off hunks. To serve the bagna cauda, you should techni-
cally have an earthenware fondue pot over an alcohol lamp, but I find
my earthenware casserole keeps the mixture hot enough for about 30
minutes without a heat source underneath. When I make this menu, I
plant everything on the table at once, even the berries in wine because
they look so pretty.

BAGNA CAUDA

8 tablespoons olive oil
5 tablespoons butter
1 2-ounce can anchovy fillets,
    drained and chopped
8 to 10 cloves garlic, chopped fine

Raw vegetables (carrot sticks,
green and/or red pepper slices,
celery sticks, fennel sticks
broccoli, cauliflower, zucchini
spears, asparagus)

In a saucepan, combine the oil, butter, anchovies, and garlic. Place
over medium heat and simmer very gently for 15 to 20 minutes or
until anchovies have melted into the oil. Eat hot as a dip for the raw
vegetables.

STRAWBERRIES IN ZINFANDEL

1 pint strawberries
2 tablespoons honey
1 cup Zinfandel wine

2 strips orange peel (2 inches long
by 1/2 inch wide)

1. Wash and hull the berries. Shake off excess water, then place
them in a serving bowl. (Clear glass makes the most impressive presentation.)

2. No more than a few hours and no less than 30 minutes before
serving, dissolve the honey in the red wine. Add the orange peel. Add
the berries and let stand at room temperature until ready to serve.

A Late Summer Feast

Grilled sweetbreads

Garlic-scented lima beans

Sliced tomatoes and onions

Ricotta, whipped cream, and peaches (see page 240)

I never think to make grilled sweetbreads except in late summer. What reminds me is the smell of them cooking at the outdoor feast of St. Gennaro just a few short blocks from my apartment in Greenwich Village. I can never bear the crowds at the feast, so I make the sweetbreads myself the way one of the vendors once showed me. Before them or with them I always have tomatoes, which I try to eat every day during their season.

GRILLED SWEETBREADS

1 pound sweetbreads	*Salt*
1 teaspoon vinegar in cold water	*1 teaspoon dried thyme*
Lightly salted water	*8 to 10 slices smoked bacon*
Fresh-ground black pepper	*(preferably nitrate-free)*

1. Soak the sweetbreads in a bowl of cold water with 1 teaspoon vinegar for 1 hour. Drain.

2. In a small saucepan, cook the sweetbreads in lightly salted water for 5 minutes. Drain and allow to cool.

3. Remove the bits of fat from the sweetbreads along with any coarse membrane. Leave on the thin membrane that keeps the lobes of the sweetbreads together.

4. Cut the sweetbreads into approximately 3-inch-long pieces. Season liberally with pepper and lightly with salt. Crush the thyme between your fingers and sprinkle all over the sweetbreads.

5. Wrap a piece of bacon around each sweetbread, trying to enclose

as much as possible, if not the whole. Secure bacon to sweetbreads with toothpicks or small trussing skewers.

6. Place as far away as possible from the heat in a gas or electric broiler. Cook about 15 minutes, turning twice. (Of course, these are even better cooked over charcoal on a barbecue or hibachi.) *Makes 2 generous servings.*

GARLIC-SCENTED LIMA BEANS

3 tablespoons olive oil
2 large cloves, garlic, peeled
1 10-ounce box frozen baby lima
  beans, thawed enough to
  separate

Salt and fresh-ground pepper
  to taste

1. In a small saucepan, over low heat, combine the olive oil and whole garlic cloves. Cook until garlic is well browned, but not burned, on all sides. Remove garlic.

2. Add lima beans and stir to coat with oil. Cook uncovered over medium heat, tossing frequently, until lima beans are creamy in center and skins are slightly crisp. Season to taste with salt and pepper and serve immediately. *Makes 2 generous servings.*

SLICED TOMATOES AND ONIONS

Slice tomatoes and onions about 1/4-inch thick and arrange them alternately and slightly overlapping on a plate. Sprinkle with salt, fresh-ground pepper, and some chopped fresh basil or parsley, if desired. Drizzle on some olive oil and serve.

Two Menus for Liver Lovers

Menu A

Risi e bisi

Sautéed calf's liver with onions and herbs

Endive salad, oil and vinegar dressing

Fresh fruit and cheese

More for its amusing sounding name than because it is extraordinary, which it isn't, risi e bisi is one of the best-known Venetian dishes. When it is well made, it is comforting like mashed potatoes with lots of butter, which is another dish which goes very well with liver. Instead of following it with the traditional Venetian strips of calf's liver with onions, for which recipes abound, try the following inauthentic variation.

RISI E BISI

2 tablespoons butter
1 slice bacon or prosciutto, chopped fine
1 small onion, chopped fine
3 cups chicken broth
3/4 cup rice (preferably imported Italian or short-grain rice)
1 10-ounce box frozen tiny peas
(without butter sauce), defrosted
Salt to taste
1/3 cup fresh-grated Parmesan cheese
2 tablespoons fine-chopped parsley
1 tablespoon butter (optional)

1. In a 2- to 3-quart saucepan, melt the butter over medium heat and sauté bacon or prosciutto with the onion until onion is golden.

2. Add broth, cover and bring to a boil. Gradually add the rice, stirring with a wooden spoon. Cover and simmer until rice is just tender, about 15 minutes. Three to five minutes before the rice is done, stir in the peas.

3. Gently stir in the cheese, parsley, and optional butter. Correct seasoning, remove from heat and let stand a minute or two before serving. Dish should be loose, but not soupy. It is eaten with a fork.

SAUTÉED CALF'S LIVER WITH ONIONS AND HERBS

2 medium onions, sliced thin	3 tablespoons fine-chopped
3 tablespoons olive oil	parsley
1 large clove garlic, chopped	Salt and fresh-ground black
fine	pepper to taste
1 heaping teaspoon dried leaf	3/4 pound calf's liver, sliced no
sage	thicker than 1/4 inch

1. Cut the onions in half through the root end, remove root, then slice thin into crescent pieces.

2. In an 8- to 10-inch skillet, heat oil over medium heat. Add onion, garlic, and sage. Sauté until onions are very tender and golden, about 15 minutes. Add parsley and sauté another minute or so. Season to taste with salt and pepper. (May be prepared in advance to this point.)

3. Pat the liver slices dry with paper toweling. Push onions to the side of the skillet and raise heat to high. Sauté the liver slices for about 30 seconds per side, seasoning each side to taste with salt and pepper. Arrange liver on a platter and place onions on top.

Menu B

Spinach-ricotta gnocchi

Sautéed liver with vinegar sauce

Baked tomatoes

Fresh fruit and cheese

The height of tomato season is the only time the tomato dish here is worth preparing. Slow and long baking does concentrate the tomatoes' flavor considerably, but the cottony tomatoes generally available can never come near the flavor of local vine-ripened fruit. If you are preparing the rest of the menu when tomatoes are out of season, substitute another vegetable, perhaps cherry tomatoes dressed with a vinaigrette sauce.

And for those who may think making gnocchi or dumplings is beyond their scope, the following recipe has only one pitfall — the spinach must be thoroughly drained of all moisture. This is easiest to do by taking a fistful at a time and squeezing it firmly over the sink. The gnocchi can even be made a day or two ahead and heated in the oven at the last minute. There are many recipes for spinach gnocchi, but this is the simplest and perhaps easiest I've come across. It is adapted from Giuliano Bugialli's *Fine Art of Italian Cooking*. In his family they are called *ravioli nudi* and I don't think Giuliano approves of my calling them *gnocchi*.

SPINACH AND RICOTTA GNOCCHI

1 package frozen chopped spinach	1/8 teaspoon fresh-grated nutmeg
1/4 cup ricotta	Salted water
2 egg yolks	3/4 cup all-purpose flour
1/2 cup fresh-grated Parmesan cheese	3 tablespoons butter
Salt and fresh-ground pepper to taste	1/4 cup fresh-grated Parmesan cheese

1. Follow package directions for cooking the spinach. Let cool slightly, then take the spinach in small handfuls and squeeze it dry.

2. In a mixing bowl, stir together the spinach, ricotta, egg yolks and Parmesan cheese. Season with salt, pepper, and nutmeg. (Can be prepared ahead to this point, refrigerated, and formed later.)

3. Bring a 3-quart saucepan of salted water to a boil.

4. Meanwhile, spread the flour on a dinner plate. Take a tablespoon of the spinach and cheese mixture and roll it in the flour into a ball. It should be compact and uniformly floured.

5. When the water is boiling, drop this first ball in as a test. It should retain its shape and rise to the top, cooked, after a minute or two or three. (If it falls apart you have left too much water in the spinach. To save the dish add a teaspoon or so of flour to the raw mixture.)

6. Before boiling the remaining ravioli nudi, use the 3 tablespoons of butter to grease a small heat-proof serving or baking dish very generously. Place the dish near the saucepan.

7. Proceed to make all the ravioli nudi. As they rise to the top cooked, lift them out of the water with a slotted spoon and place in the buttered dish. Sprinkle with remaining Parmesan cheese and serve immediately. (Giuliano doesn't recommend it, but I've found these can be made ahead without the last sprinkling of cheese, covered and kept perfectly in the refrigerator. Place covered with foil in a 350° oven to reheat.)

SAUTÉED LIVER WITH VINEGAR SAUCE

3/4 pound beef or calf's liver, sliced thin
Salt and fresh-ground black pepper
Flour
2 tablespoons butter

2 teaspoons red-wine vinegar
1/4 cup dry white wine or vermouth
1 teaspoon bottled meat glaze or beef bouillon crystals

1. With a sharp knife or scissors, cut the liver into strips about 3 inches long. Season with salt and pepper.

2. Place some flour on a plate or piece of waxed paper, dredge the liver slices lightly, shaking off excess flour.

3. In a large skillet, melt the butter over medium-high heat and quickly sauté the liver slices until browned. As the pieces are done, remove to a plate.

4. Add vinegar and wine to skillet, scraping up any browned bits. Add meat glaze or bouillon crystals and mix well. Return liver to skillet and cook just long enough to turn the slices in the sauce. Serve immediately.

BAKED TOMATOES

2 large tomatoes
1/3 cup olive oil
2 tablespoons fine-chopped
  parsley

2 to 3 large cloves garlic, chopped
  very fine
Salt and fresh-ground pepper to
  taste

1. Wash the tomatoes and cut them in half. Place in a baking dish just large enough to hold them (a 9- or 10-inch pie plate is usually perfect).

2. Sprinkle the parsley and garlic evenly over the tomatoes, pressing them in with your fingers slightly. Pour the olive oil over the tomatoes, letting it run into the baking dish. Season with salt and pepper.

3. Place tomatoes in a preheated 425° oven until the oil starts to sizzle. Baste the tomatoes with oil from the baking dish and lower heat to 300°. Bake until tomatoes have completely collapsed, about 1 hour, basting them several times. Do not worry if they blacken somewhat. Serve hot or, even better, at room temperature.

A Dinner for Valentine's Day

Veal Andrea
Peas with scallions
More-than-fried potatoes
Oranges jubilee

It's difficult to be romantic at the table when you're busy at the stove, even when the stove is in the same room. Here, then, is a menu that can be prepared almost entirely in advance. The only real last-minute work, other than final heating, is the flaming of the dessert. That you can do, with much bravado and a little pretention, right in front of your guest.

VEAL ANDREA

4 veal cutlets (or chicken or
   turkey cutlets)
1/2 cup flour
2 tablespoons butter
1/2 pound mushrooms, sliced
   thin
1/4 teaspoon dried leaf sage,
   crumbled

3/4 cup dry white wine
Salt and pepper to taste
6 ounces pound Fontina cheese,
   shredded
4 slices prosciutto ham

1. Pat cutlets dry with absorbent paper. Place flour on a dinner plate, dredge cutlets, and shake off excess flour.

2. In a skillet, heat butter. Over high heat, sauté cutlets on each side for 30 seconds. Set aside on a plate.

3. In the same skillet, sauté the mushrooms over medium heat until they give off their liquid. Add the sage, raise the heat slightly, and cook until mushroom liquid has evaporated.

4. Add the white wine, about 1/4 teaspoon salt and 2 to 3 grindings of black pepper. Cook over medium-high heat until all but a few tablespoons of liquid have evaporated. Correct seasoning if necessary.

5. In a baking pan just large enough to hold the cutlets (a 9- or 10-inch pie plate may do), place about half the mushrooms. Place the cutlets over them.

6. Sprinkle half the cheese over the cutlets, then place a slice of ham over each cutlet. Divide the remaining mushrooms over the cutlets, then top with the remaining cheese. Set aside or cover and refrigerate until ready to finish cooking, about 20 minutes before serving.

7. Bake in a preheated 375° oven for 20 minutes or until cheese is melted and sauce is bubbling in the bottom of the dish. Serve immediately.

PEAS WITH SCALLIONS

2 tablespoons butter
4 scallions (use only white and
   light green parts), sliced thin

1 10-ounce box frozen tiny peas
   (petits pois)
Salt and pepper to taste

1. In a small saucepan, heat the butter. Over medium heat, sauté the sliced scallions about 2 minutes. Add the frozen peas and toss in the butter. Season to taste. Refrigerate until ready to finish cooking, about 5 minutes before serving.

2. About 5 minutes before serving, place the peas over medium heat, uncovered and with no additional water. Cook for 5 to 7 minutes or until peas are just tender, stirring occasionally.

MORE-THAN-FRIED POTATOES

2 Idaho baking potatoes about
   5 inches long

Vegetable oil

1. Peel the potatoes, then cut into strips about 1/2-inch thick and wide.

2. Bring a saucepan of salted water to a boil, then add potato strips. Cover saucepan so water will return to a boil quickly and cook potatoes exactly 5 minutes from time water returns to a boil.

3. Drain potatoes, then dry with absorbent paper. (So you won't clutter the kitchen, arrange paper towels or brown paper on a baking sheet or other flat surface you can carry out to another room.)

4. In a large skillet, heat about 1/8-inch layer of oil until a drop of water bounces on it. Arrange the potatoes in the skillet and fry over medium-high heat, turning often, until all sides are well browned. Drain on absorbent paper. (Again, do this on a transportable surface.) Do not clean the skillet; reserve for final crisping of the potatoes.

5. Immediately before serving, crisp the potatoes in the same skillet. Heat oil to almost smoking, add potatoes, and turn quickly in the hot oil until crisp.

ORANGES JUBILEE

1 11-ounce can mandarin orange
   segments in light syrup
2 tablespoons sugar
2 tablespoons orange liqueur

2 teaspoons cornstarch
1 pint vanilla ice cream
2 to 3 tablespoons orange liqueur

1. Drain the can of oranges, pouring the liquid directly into a small saucepan.

2. Blend the sugar, 2 tablespoons of orange liqueur, and cornstarch into the syrup. Place over medium heat and stir constantly until sugar is dissolved and sauce thickens. (May be prepared in advance to this point. Also spoon ice cream into serving dishes and place in freezer until ready to serve.)

3. Just before serving, add the orange segments and heat the sauce through. Heat the 2 to 3 tablespoons orange liqueur in a 1/4-cup metal measuring cup. Pour the sauce and orange slices over the ice cream. Ignite the heated liqueur and pour some over each serving. Serve immediately.

Tripe for Two on a Spring Evening

Cheese and anchovy spiedini

Tripe in lemon sauce

Asparagus baked with butter and a fresh herb

Fresh strawberries dipped into sugar then into lightly whipped cream

A feast to bind a relationship based on an unusual and mutual fondness for one of the least romantic of foods, cow's stomach.

SPIEDINI ALLA ROMANA (SKEWERED CHEESE SANDWICHES)

6 1/2-inch thick slices Italian
   bread, toasted
8 whole anchovy fillets

1/2 pound mozzarella cheese in
   4 slices
6 tablespoons olive oil

1. Spear 3 slices of bread, 2 slices of cheese, and 4 anchovy fillets on two skewers as if they were triple-decker sandwiches. Between each pair of bread slices, there should be 2 anchovies and a slice of cheese.

2. Place each skewer on an individual ovenproof dish greased with a tablespoon of oil, or put both in a small oiled baking dish. (May be prepared ahead to this point.)

3. Place in a preheated 400° oven until cheese is melted. Serve immediately, drizzled with the remaining 4 tablespoons oil.

TRIPE IN LEMON SAUCE

1 pound precleaned tripe
1 carrot
1 medium onion
1 rib celery
5 tablespoons olive oil

2 medium onions, sliced
Salt and fresh-ground black
   pepper to taste
2 egg yolks
Juice of 1/2 lemon

1. In a 3-quart or larger saucepan, combine the tripe, carrot, onion, and celery. Cover well with boiling water, cover and bring back to the boil. Boil for about 1-1/2 to 2 hours or until tender enough to eat. (Cut off a little piece and taste for tenderness.) Drain well. Discard the vegetables.

2. Cut the tripe into 3-inch long by 3/8-inch wide strips. Set aside. (May be prepared ahead to this point. Can be refrigerated for up to two days.)

3. In a large skillet, heat the oil and sauté onions over medium heat. When the onions are just wilted, about 4 minutes, add the tripe. Stir-

ring frequently, sauté over medium heat for 10 minutes without browning. Season to taste with salt and pepper.

4. Meanwhile, in a small bowl or cup, beat the egg yolks and lemon juice together.

5. Remove tripe from heat, wait until oil stops sizzling, then quickly stir in the egg yolk mixture. Egg yolks should thicken and coat the tripe and onions without curdling. Serve immediately.

ASPARAGUS BAKED WITH BUTTER AND A FRESH HERB

1 pound asparagus
4 tablespoons butter
1 teaspoon salt
A few sprigs of fresh tarragon,

chervil, dill, mint, parsley, or al-most any other fresh herb that is available

(For this menu, a pound of asparagus is probably not too much. But if you think it is, you can make less.)

1. Wash the asparagus well and cut off the tough bottoms. And if you want to be more thoughtful of aesthetics than nutrition, peel the bottom halves with a swivel-bladed vegetable peeler. (I find thinner asparagus doesn't need peeling.)

2. Place the asparagus in a baking dish, dot with butter, place the herb on top, and cover tightly with foil or the cover to the dish. (May be prepared ahead to this point.)

3. Place in a preheated 350° oven for 20 to 30 minutes, depending on size of asparagus and whether you intend to eat them hot or at room temperature. If serving at room temperature, undercook the asparagus to allow for continued cooking while they cool. May be served hot or just warm and can be eaten, rather messily but sensuously, with the fingers.

STRAWBERRIES WITH SUGAR AND CREAM

1 cup heavy cream　　　　　*Bowl of extra fine or powdered*
1 pint strawberries　　　　　*sugar*

1. The cream should not be sweetened and should not be whipped more than a few hours in advance. Whip only until the cream is thick enough to form a ribbon that doesn't dissolve when dripped off the beaters.

2. Wash the berries just before serving and do not remove the stems or leaves.

3. Serve the berries in their basket or a bowl, the whipped cream and sugar in separate bowls. Dip the strawberries by hand into each.

A Quick Chinese Dinner

Fried meat cakes

Egg foo yung

Boiled rice

Fresh fruit or ice cream

Both the meat cakes and the egg foo yung can be made in the same pot—a Chinese wok or large cast-iron casserole. You may even include the oil from cooking the meat in the oil for cooking the egg foo yung. And, of course, almost any diced leftovers can be tossed into the egg mixture instead of the ingredients listed. And, especially considering there is a meat appetizer, you could make it entirely with vegetables.

FRIED MEAT CAKES

1/2 pound ground beef
2 teaspoons dry sherry
1 teaspoon dark brown sugar
2 teaspoons soy sauce
1 clove garlic, crushed

1 egg
2 teaspoons cornstarch
Dash salt
Dash black pepper
1/2 cup vegetable oil.

1. In a bowl, combine all the ingredients except the oil. Beat with a spoon or knead by hand until very well blended. Chill for at least 20 minutes.

2. In a wok or large casserole, heat the oil over medium-high heat. Drop the meat mixture by rounded tablespoonfuls into the hot fat and fry until browned on both sides. Drain on absorbent paper. May be served hot or at room temperature. *Makes about a dozen small cakes.*

EGG FOO YUNG

For sauce:
1 cup chicken or vegetable
    bouillon
1 teaspoon ketchup
1 tablespoon soy sauce
1-1/2 tablespoons cornstarch
1/4 cup cold water

For pancakes:
3/4 cup diced roast pork, roast
    beef, cooked chicken, or shrimp
1/3 cup diced celery
1/4 cup diced scallion
1/3 cup diced green pepper
5 eggs
1/2 teaspoon salt
1 teaspoon dry sherry
Dash black pepper
1 cup vegetable oil

1. To make sauce, which should be done in advance or just before preparing pancakes, in a small saucepan combine the broth, ketchup, and soy sauce. Bring to a simmer. Dissolve cornstarch in water, stir into sauce, and continue stirring until smooth and thickened. Pour over pancakes and serve.

2. In a mixing bowl, combine all the pancake ingredients. With chopsticks or a spoon, stir to mix well, but do not beat.

3. In a wok or deep pot, such as a Dutch oven, heat half the oil over medium heat. Using a large kitchen spoon or ladle, scoop about a quarter of the egg mixture into the oil. (If wok or pot is large enough, make two pancakes at a time.) When the edges are brown, turn the pancake over. (This is most easily done with two spoons or a spoon and a spatula.) Brown the other side.

4. Remove the pancake with a slotted spoon so the oil will drain off; place on a heatproof platter lined with absorbent paper and set in a warm oven. Continue to make pancakes, adding more oil as necessary.

A Hot or Cold Dinner

Whole boiled artichokes, lemon butter or lemon dressing
Baked salmon steaks with dill or green garlic and caper sauce
Armenian pilaf or rice salad (see pages 114 and 50)
Chinese almond float (see page 237)

The menu is oriented toward spring, when weather and moods tend to change suddenly. You can have a hot meal if you want to bother with last-minute cooking or you can have a cold meal if you want or are forced to prepare ahead. Picking artichokes apart petal by petal can be an erotic undertaking, by the way.

BOILED ARTICHOKES

2 firm, large artichokes   1/4 teaspoon salt
1 lemon, cut in half

1. Wash artichokes under cold water, making sure water runs between leaves.

2. With a sharp knife, cut off the stems at the base and remove the small bottom leaves and any discolored or particularly tough-looking outer leaves. As you are cutting, rub lemon juice over the cut surfaces to prevent them from discoloring.

3. With scissors, snip off the pointed ends of the outside leaves. With a sharp knife, cut off the top 1/2 to 1-inch of the artichokes. (This last step is optional.)

4. After each artichoke is prepared for cooking, put it in a large bowl of cold water to which you have added the juice of half the lemon.

5. Stand artichokes in a saucepan just large enough to hold them, snugly if possible. Add enough water to come about 2 to 3 inches up the side of the pan. Add salt, cover, and bring to a boil.

6. Boil for 30 to 45 minutes or until the bases can be pierced with a fork. If serving cold, undercook slightly. Remove from saucepan and drain upside down.

7. To remove inedible choke and prickly inner leaves, gently spread the leaves apart and pull out the cone of purple-tinged leaves, then gently scrape out choke hairs located on top of the meaty "bottom" with a teaspoon. Serve warm or cold with a dipping sauce.

BAKED SALMON STEAKS

2 tablespoons butter
2 1-1/2-inch thick salmon steaks, each weighing about 10 ounces
Salt and fresh-ground black pepper

1/4 cup lemon juice (2 lemons)
4 tablespoons butter

1. Using 2 tablespoons butter, generously grease a baking dish just large enough to hold the salmon steaks.

2. Season the steaks with salt and pepper, then place in the baking dish. Pour the lemon juice over the salmon, then dot with the remaining butter.

3. Bake in a preheated 400° oven for about 20 minutes or until fish will flake, basting frequently with the pan juices. Sprinkle with chopped fresh dill and serve immediately. Or cool to room temperature, then refrigerate and serve cold on a bed of spinach or lettuce with garlic dip (page 201).

A Romantic Summer Dinner

Cold crab bisque (see Page 14)
Shrimp Remoulade on a bed of spinach
Hot sweet corn, sweet butter
Pound cake Sauternes

A perfect menu for late summer beach days when, at a farm stand, you can buy corn picked that day and enjoy it, at home, with cold seafood prepared the day before. This is a rather extravagant meal, but, as a friend of mine says, "If it's not labor-intensive, it has to be capital-intensive." However, don't go to the expense of buying a full-sized bottle of Sauterne. Buy the best you can afford—Château Coutet or a Château Climens perhaps—but only a half-bottle. That's plenty for two.

SHRIMP REMOULADE

1/4 cup Dijon mustard
2 teaspoons sweet paprika
1/2 to 1 teaspoon cayenne pepper
1 teaspoon salt
1/2 cup wine vinegar
1 cup olive oil
1-1/2 cups coarse-chopped scallions (including part of the
green)
1/2 cup fine-chopped celery
1/2 cup fine-chopped parsley
1-1/2 to 2 pounds shrimp
Spinach leaves (about 1/2 pound)

1. In a mixing bowl, with a wire whisk or electric hand mixer, beat together the mustard, cayenne, paprika, and salt.

2. Add the vinegar gradually, still beating, then slowly add the olive oil, continuously beating.

3. Stir in the scallions, celery, and parsley.

4. Shell and devein any shrimp that have obvious black lines running down their back.

5. Bring a large pot of water to a boil and add the shrimp. Cook just until they turn pink, usually in about the time it takes the water to return to a boil, about 2 minutes. Drain thoroughly.

6. While still warm, toss the shrimp in the sauce in the mixing bowl. Cover and refrigerate at least 12 hours or until ready to serve.

7. To serve, arrange beds of spinach leaves on two plates. Arrange the shrimp on top of the spinach and pour some of the sauce over the shrimp. Serve remaining sauce separately.

An Inauthentic Indian Dinner

Cherry tomatoes with bowls of vodka, curry, and coarse salt

Tandoori chicken (see page 121)

Rice with peanuts

Green salad

Lassi   Fresh fruit

Food writers have been saying for years that curry powder is not an Indian, but a British, invention. In India, they tell us, curry is a kind of dish and the many spices that go into a curry are nonspecific — they vary from region to region and from household to household. Nevertheless, I find commercial curry powder very useful and not at all unworthy. Serve it here for seasoning cherry tomatoes after you and your guest have dipped them in vodka and before you've dipped them in salt (see page 198).

RICE WITH PEANUTS

1/2 teaspoon salt
1 cup long-grain rice

1/3 cup roasted unsalted peanuts
1 tablespoon butter

1. Bring 2 cups water and the salt to a boil. Stir in rice, cover and simmer until almost done, about 14 minutes.

2. Gently stir in the peanuts and butter with a fork, recover, and set over the lowest possible heat for another 5 minutes or until fluffy and dry. Fluff the rice with a fork before serving.

LASSI

8 ounces plain yogurt
1 cup orange juice, preferably
   fresh-squeezed
2 teaspoons honey

1/2 teaspoon rose water
1/4 teaspoon ground nutmeg,
   coriander, or cardamom (or a
   pinch of all three)

In a quart jar, combine all the ingredients and shake until well mixed. Or, in a mixing bowl, beat all ingredients together well. Or, divide ingredients between two large glasses and stir well.

An Easy, Light Romantic Dinner for Any Season

Jamaican avocados
Carpaccio (see page 67)
Baked puffed pancake

Jamaican avocados is a recipe from Shirley and Joe Pisacane, chef-owners of Periscope restaurant in Sante Fe, New Mexico. It is unusual, simple and delicious. The same can be said of carpaccio, paper-thin slices of raw beef topped with slivers of Parmesan cheese, thin-sliced mushrooms, and a lemon dressing. The puffed pancake, for which the batter can be prepared ahead, is a sweet version of Yorkshire pudding— delicious with fancy fruit preserves.

JAMAICAN AVOCADOS

2 tablespoons butter
1 tablespoon warm water
1 tablespoon red-wine vinegar
1 tablespoon sugar
1 tablespoon Worcestershire sauce
1/2 tablespoon ketchup

1/2 teaspoon dry mustard
4 whole cloves
1/4 teaspoon salt
Several dashes Tabasco sauce
1 tablespoon dark rum
1 large, ripe avocado

1. In a very small saucepan, combine all the ingredients except rum and avocado. Bring to a gentle simmer, stirring constantly. Simmer about five minutes.

2. Fish out the cloves and discard. Stir in the rum and cook sauce another 2 minutes. (May be prepared ahead and reheated.)

3. Cut the avocado in half lengthwise, then twist the halves in opposite directions to separate them. Remove the pit. With a knife, score the cut sides of the avocado lightly. Pour the warm sauce into the avocado halves and serve.

BAKED PUFFED PANCAKE

3 eggs
1/2 cup milk
1/4 cup all-purpose flour
1 tablespoon sugar
1/2 teaspoon salt

1 tablespoon butter
Lemon juice
Powdered sugar
Fruit preserves, marmalade, or
  jelly

1. To prepare batter, in a large bowl beat eggs until light. Beat in milk, flour, sugar, and salt until smooth. (This can all be done in a

blender or food processor as well.) If preparing ahead, cover with plastic and refrigerate. Beat again just before baking.

2. Place a tablespoon of butter into a 9- or 10-inch round baking dish or pie plate. Preheat oven to 450° and place baking dish in oven while it preheats, to melt butter and heat dish.

3. When butter has melted and dish is very hot, remove dish, swirl the butter around the sides of the dish, immediately replace on oven rack and pour in batter.

4. Bake for 8 minutes. Reduce heat to 375° and bake about another 8 minutes or until pancake is golden. Surface should be irregular and with high sides.

5. Immediately sprinkle with lemon juice, dust with powdered sugar, and serve. Serve with a choice of fruit preserves, marmalade, or jelly.

Dinners for Four

Even people with large kitchens like to prepare as much of the food as they can before dinnertime. It is no longer considered rude to serve simple food, but it is rude to be stuck in the kitchen for long periods after the guests have arrived. The menus in this chapter range from casual meals to enjoy with friends to formal menus for special occasions and less intimate acquaintances. All have been coordinated for preparation in a small kitchen with the introduction to each menu outlining some organization hints and suggesting solutions to any special problems the menu may present.

A Virginia Dinner

Oyster soup (see page 15)

Ham steak baked in milk

Cooked greens (see page 155) or wilted salad (see page 51)

Spoon bread or baked sweet potatoes   Sweet butter

Fruit fool (see page 235)

Ham baked in milk sounds strange to the uninitiated, but once you've tasted the dark brown crust that builds up over the tender and mildly sweet meat, it will become one of your absolute favorite recipes for ham. Spoon bread, a souffle-like cornmeal pudding, with plenty of sweet butter, is the perfect accompaniment, but both ham and spoon bread require your oven space. My answer for this small-kitchen logistics problem is to put the spoon bread in the oven the second you remove the ham. The ham is delicious even when it is no very hot, so it can wait the 30 minutes, covered with foil, while the spoon bread bakes and you enjoy your soup. If you can't manage this, or don't want the oven heating up your apartment for that long, tuck yams around the baking ham in the empty spaces on the oven rack or prepare spoon bread (see page 110) in advance. Cooked greens can be prepared ahead, in a saucepan. Or, just before serving, in a skillet, you can finish off the hot bacon and onion dressing for a wilted salad.

With this menu choose an Alsatian Gewürztraminer or a semidry California Riesling or Chenin Blanc. Beer would also be fine.

HAM STEAK BAKED IN MILK

1 1-1/4-inch thick center cut
  ham steak (about 2-1/2
  pounds)
2 teaspoons brown sugar

1/2 teaspoon dry mustard
1/4 teaspoon ground ginger
1 quart (approximately) milk

1. The ham steak should have a round center bone and about a half-inch layer of fat surrounding it. Cut off a small piece of the fat and, with it, grease a baking dish not much larger than the steak. An oblong Pyrex baking dish will do, but a gratin pan that is attractive enough to go to the table is better.

2. Rub half the brown sugar, mustard, and ginger into one side of the ham steak. Place it in the greased baking dish and rub the other side of the ham steak with the remaining flavorings.

3. Pour in enough milk just to cover the ham steak. Place in a preheated 350° oven and bake for about 2 hours. When done, all the milk will have evaporated and there will be a dark brown crust over the meat and sticking to the pan. Include a piece of this crust with each serving of meat.

COOKED GREENS

1/4 pound bacon or salt
   pork, diced
1 small onion, chopped
2 pounds fresh, trimmed and
   well washed or 2 10-ounce
   boxes frozen mustard

greens, collards, kale, or
   dandelion leaves
Red pepper flakes or hot
   pepper sauce to taste
Vinegar to taste

1. In a saucepan, combine the bacon or salt pork and onion with 3 cups of water. Cover and boil for 1 hour.

2. Add the greens. Simmer fresh greens uncovered for about 15 minutes or until tender. Cover frozen greens, bring back to a boil, break up the greens with a fork, and cook another five minutes or until tender. Season with pepper and vinegar to taste. Salt should not be necessary.

SPOON BREAD

1 cup white cornmeal
2 tablespoons butter, cut
   into small pieces
1-1/2 teaspoons salt
2 cups boiling water

4 egg yolks
1/2 cup milk
1/2 cup flour
4 teaspoons baking powder
4 egg whites

1. In a mixing bowl, combine the cornmeal, butter, and salt. Pour in the boiling water and stir until butter is melted. Let cool slightly.

2. Beat in the egg yolks and milk, then the flour and baking powder.

3. In another bowl, beat the egg whites until stiff peaks form. Fold egg whites into batter, then pour into a greased 2-quart casserole. Bake in a preheated 375° oven for 30 minutes. Serve immediately. *Makes 4 to 6 servings.* (Leftovers may be reheated the next day as corn bread or dried out and crumbled for pork chop stuffing.)

A Middle Eastern Feast for the Hot Weather

Tuna packed in olive oil; Imported green and black olives; Feta
cheese; Pickled peppers; Pickled onions

Lamb in yogurt sauce

Tabouleh salad (see page 60)   Sautéed zucchini

Fruit sherbet

Dried fruits and nuts

The appetizers here, to be served with cocktails or wine before set-
tling down to dinner, can perhaps be purchased in jars or cans at very
large supermarkets or from a good specialty food store. Arrange them
all together on a large platter or in individual dishes with radishes and
carrot sticks, green and red pepper strips and slices of tomato. Good
bread is a must.

The lamb, except for its final garlic-mint fillip, can be prepared
well ahead and because the meat is not browned you won't have to
stand in a hot kitchen while it's cooking. The cold tabouleh can also
be done far ahead, and room temperature zucchini are even better
than hot. The whole meal can be done at leisure and won't overheat
your apartment. For a change chill a light red wine very well—a Beaujolais, Côte du Rhône, young Chianti, or Zinfandel.

LAMB IN YOGURT

1-1/2 pounds lean, boneless
  lamb, cut into 1-inch cubes
1 medium onion, chopped
  fine
1/2 cup water
1 teaspoon salt
1/4 teaspoon fresh-ground
  black pepper
1-1/2 cups plain yogurt

1 tablespoon cornstarch
1 egg
2 cloves garlic, mashed
1 tablespoon fine-chopped
  fresh mint or 1-1/2
  teaspoons ground dried
  mint
1 tablespoon butter

1. In a 3-quart saucepan, combine the lamb, onion, water, salt, and pepper. Bring to a simmer, cover and simmer very gently until meat is tender, about 1 hour.

2. In a small bowl, beat together the yogurt, cornstarch, and egg. Stir into the meat mixture and, stirring constantly, cook until sauce is thickened and smooth. (If preparing ahead to this point, add the yogurt mixture, stir well, but do not continue to cook. Reheat, then cook until thickened and smooth before continuing.)

3. In your smallest skillet, sauté the garlic and mint in the butter for just a minute. Scrape into the lamb stew, stir and serve immediately.

SAUTÉED ZUCCHINI

2 tablespoons butter
1 tablespoon vegetable oil
4 medium zucchini squashes,
    sliced 1/4-inch thick

Salt and pepper to taste

In a large skillet, heat the butter and oil together over medium-high heat. Sauté the zucchini, gently tossing them frequently. Do not allow zucchini to become mushy. Season with salt and pepper. Place in a serving bowl and let stand at room temperature until ready to eat.

An Informal French Provençal Dinner for Late Summer

Ratatouille   Crusty bread

Chicken baked with 40 cloves of garlic

Green salad

Linzertorte (see page 224)

Being a city dweller, I depend mostly on the vegetable market for my produce. But, at the end of summer, all my suburban friends with vegetable gardens start to palm off their excesses on me. With the freshly picked tomatoes, eggplant, and squash they give me, I indulge in a large batch of ratatouille, at least double the recipe here. If you have garden-fresh ingredients and a pot that's large enough, I recommend you do it, too. It keeps well enough for about 10 days and can be eaten hot, warm, or cold, as an appetizer, a side dish, a vegetable bed for broiled chops or sausage, an omelet or crepe filling, or with a piece of cheese and a hunk of bread for a quick meal.

In the chicken dish, here again is garlic in its more tamed condition, although it remains a penetrating flavor. When I first made this dish, everyone liked the flavor of the meat, but not the look of the chicken skin, which remains white like boiled chicken. Therefore, I now remove the skin. Continue the bread through the chicken course. You'll need it to sop up the cooking juices. A Beaujolais, Côte du Rhône, or California Petit Sirah should wash the ratatouille and chicken down nicely.

RATATOUILLE

1/4 cup olive oil
1 medium onion
2 to 3 cloves garlic, chopped fine
1 medium eggplant, washed but not peeled, cut into 1/2-inch cubes
1 medium yellow or green summer squash, washed but not peeled, cut into 1/2-inch cubes

1 large green pepper and 1 large red pepper (or 2 of one), washed, seeded, and cut into 1/2-inch strips
3 medium tomatoes, peeled, seeded, and cut into 1/2-inch cubes
Salt and fresh-ground black pepper to taste

1. In a large skillet with cover, heat the oil and sauté onions over medium heat until tender but not browned. Add the garlic and sauté a minute longer.

2. Add the eggplant, squash, and peppers. Sprinkle with salt and

pepper to taste and toss in the oil just to mix the vegetables and coat lightly with oil.

3. Lower heat and cover skillet. Cook over low heat about 30 minutes or until vegetables are tender but still holding their shape.

4. Add the tomato and raise heat to medium. Cover and cook for about 5 minutes. Uncover, raise heat to high, and cook briskly 5 more minutes. Taste and correct seasoning before serving.

CHICKEN BAKED WITH 40 CLOVES OF GARLIC

1 cup olive oil
40 cloves garlic
3/4 teaspoon each of dried
   rosemary, thyme, and sage
5 sprigs parsley
2 ribs celery (with tops if
   possible), cut in half

1 4-pound roasting chicken,
   quartered and skinned
Salt and fresh-ground black
   pepper to taste

1. In a Dutch oven or earthenware casserole large enough to hold all the chicken, place the olive oil, garlic, herbs, parsley, and celery. Let stand at least 20 minutes.

2. Meanwhile, wash the chicken quarters and dry well with paper towels. Sprinkle chicken generously with salt and pepper.

3. One piece at a time, place the chicken in the pot and roll it around in the oil mixture until completely coated. When all the chicken is in the pot, cover with a piece of aluminum foil, then the tight-fitting cover. (Traditionally, the pot is sealed with a flour-and-water paste.)

4. Bake in a preheated 325° oven for 1-1/2 hours without ever taking the cover off.

5. Open pot and arrange chicken on a warm platter. Cover with the foil to keep warm.

6. Remove the garlic and squeeze each piece between the fingers to free each clove from its skin. Discard the skins. In a small bowl, with

a fork, mash garlic into a paste, then mix with about 1 cup of the juices from the pot. Serve in a sauceboat with the chicken. (Any left-over juices from the pot will make a delicious sauce for pasta at an-other meal.)

A Steak Dinner

Snails in mushroom caps

Flank steak with whole-pepper marinade

Orange-glazed carrot ribbons

Watercress and endive salad with mustard dressing (see page 47)

Roquefort cheese   Sauterne

Oatmeal lace cookies (see page 229)   Coffee

Eating snails from shells, as they are most commonly served, is often difficult, even if you have those special plates with indentations, snail tongs, and tiny forks. I'm also always worried that reusing the shells is unsanitary because I can't see what's doing inside them. In any case, serving snails in mushroom caps looks just as impressive and one gets to eat the snail container as well.

As far as I know, snails can be purchased only in cans in this coun-try. I used to get tiny, live land snails in some Italian markets, but these are getting more difficult to come by and are too small for this presentation, anyway.

The steak is a simple marinated and broiled affair. The carrot rib-bons are something dreamed up in the days when I hated cooked carrots but seemed to know somebody who didn't. Serve the salad with the meat course or after it, as you wish, since this is a difficult menu for fine wine, anyway. The spiciness of the steak and the sweet-ness of the carrots will interfere with your appreciation of a wine's subtleties. I'd suggest serving a good California jug wine (out of a carafe) with the meat, then surprise everyone with a first-rate French sauterne served with a separate course of authentic Roquefort cheese, a delectable pairing of two aggressive flavors.

SNAILS IN MUSHROOM CAPS

*1/4 pound butter, at room
  temperature
1 large shallot, chopped fine
2 to 3 large cloves garlic,
  chopped fine
2 heaping tablespoons fine-
  chopped parsley
Scant 1/2 teaspoon salt*

*1/4 teaspoon fresh-ground
  black pepper
12 large mushrooms, stems
  removed
Olive oil
12 canned large snails
4 slices toasted bread*

1. In a small bowl, cream the butter with a fork, then add the shallot, garlic, parsley, salt, and pepper. Mix very well. (May be prepared ahead.)

2. Brush the mushroom caps with olive oil. Or, if you haven't a brush, roll them in oil poured into a small plate or bowl. Arrange the caps in a baking dish.

3. Place a snail and a rounded teaspoon of butter in each cap. (May be prepared ahead to this point.) Bake in preheated 375° oven for about 20 minutes. Serve mushrooms on toast to absorb the butter.

FLANK STEAK WITH WHOLE-PEPPER MARINADE

*1 tablespoon black
  peppercorns
1 2- to 2-1/2-pound flank
  steak, well trimmed
1 small onion, sliced
2 cloves garlic, sliced
1 large bay leaf, broken into
  pieces*

*2 to 3 sprigs parsley
1 cup dry red wine
1 tablespoon olive oil
1/2 teaspoon salt
1 tablespoon cognac
Olive oil*

1. Wrap the peppercorns in the corner of a clean dish towel, then, with a mallet or the bottom of a heavy water tumbler, crack the peppercorns coarse.

2. Massage the cracked peppercorns in both sides of the steak. Strew the onions, garlic, bay leaf, and parsley on the bottom of a shallow glass or enameled baking dish and place the steak on top, folding over the end of the steak if it is too long for the dish.

3. Combine the remaining ingredients and pour over the steak. Turn the steak in the marinade and marinate in the refrigerator for 24 hours, turning once or twice.

4. Before grilling, remove the steak from the marinade and pat dry, leaving whatever peppercorns stick to the meat, but removing any bits of garlic, onion, parsley, or bay leaf. Brush lightly with olive oil.

5. Grill close to the heat in a gas or electric broiler until done to taste.

ORANGE-GLAZED CARROT RIBBONS

1 pound carrots	Fresh-ground black pepper
4 tablespoons butter	to taste
1/2 teaspoon salt	1/2 cup orange juice

1. With a swivel-bladed vegetable peeler, scrape the carrots. Then, using medium pressure with the peeler, make carrot ribbons by cutting the carrots into lengthwise strips, rotating the carrot as you go.

2. In a large skillet, melt the butter over medium-high heat and sauté carrots for about 2 minutes. Season with salt and pepper.

3. Add the orange juice, stir well, reduce heat to medium, and cover skillet. Let carrots steam in the juice for about 3 minutes.

4. Uncover and continue to cook over medium-high heat, tossing the carrots constantly, for about 2 more minutes or until liquid has mostly evaporated and left a syrupy glaze on the carrots. Serve immediately.

A Seafood Dinner

Pan roast of clams in the style of the Grand Central Oyster Bar

Fish baked in paper with a vegetable melange

Creamy rice pudding (see page 234)

This menu has just three dishes with no accompaniments. But since the rich pan roast can virtually stand on its own as a main course, the baked fish has a vegetable stuffing, and the custardy rice pudding is plenty starchy, there's more than enough food here for big appetites. Serve with a California Chardonnay or Sauvignon Blanc.

PAN ROAST OF CLAMS IN THE STYLE OF THE GRAND CENTRAL OYSTER BAR

---

4 tablespoons butter
4 teaspoons Worcestershire
  sauce
1/2 cup bottled chili sauce
1 tablespoon sweet paprika
1/4 teaspoon Tabasco sauce
4 dozen shucked littleneck
  or cherrystone clams, with
  their juice

1 quart half-and-half (or half
  heavy cream and half
  milk)
8 1/2-inch-thick slices
  Italian or French bread,
  dried in the oven

1. In a 3-quart saucepan, melt the butter over medium heat. Stir in the Worcestershire sauce, chili sauce, paprika, and Tabasco. (May be prepared ahead to this point.)

2. Bring to a simmer, then add the clams with their juice. Cook over medium heat, stirring constantly, until mixture begins to simmer again, about another minute.

3. Stir in the half-and-half. When mixture is heated through and just beginning to simmer, remove from heat and serve in bowls over dry bread.

FISH BAKED IN PAPER WITH A
VEGETABLE MELANGE

1 whole 3- to 4-pound
   weakfish (sea trout),
   bluefish, or bass
Salt and fresh-ground
   black pepper
1/2 cup chopped scallions
   or spring onions (white part
   only)
1 medium green pepper, diced

1/2 cup thin-sliced celery
2 medium potatoes, peeled
2 carrots, scraped
3 tablespoons fine-chopped
   parsley
1/4 teaspoon dried tarragon
1 teaspoon salt
3 tablespoons fine-chopped
   into small bits

1. If desired, have the fish boned for stuffing. (Ideally, it should be cooked with its head, but have the head removed if you find it looks too unappetizing.) Season the fish inside and out with salt and pepper. Set aside.

2. In a large bowl, place the scallions, green pepper, and celery. Using the coarse side of a four-sided hand grater, shred the potatoes and carrots directly into the bowl. Add parsley, tarragon, and salt. Toss well.

3. Put 1 cup of the vegetable mixture in the center of an oiled piece of baking parchment or aluminum foil twice the length of the fish. Dot with a few pieces of butter. Place the fish on the bed of vegetables and stuff the fish with about another cup of vegetable mixture and a few more dots of butter.

4. Place the remaining vegetables on top of the fish, dot with remaining butter and fold the parchment or foil to form a tight, neat bundle. If using parchment, use string to tie the package, if necessary. (May be prepared several hours ahead to this point. Refrigerate until ready to bake.)

5. Place the package on a baking sheet or in a baking pan in a preheated 350° oven for 50 minutes. To serve, carefully place the whole package on a serving platter and open it at the table. (Use scissors on the parchment. You may tear the foil.)

A Westernized Japanese Chicken Dinner

Thick rice soup (see page 20)
Teriyaki chicken
Cucumber salad
Fresh orange salad (see page 181)

This is an informal menu for everyday family meals, and beer is in order. The most appropriate would, of course, be Kirin or other beer from Japan.

TERIYAKI CHICKEN

1/4 cup honey
1/4 cup dry sherry
1/2 cup soy sauce
1/4 cup water
1/4 teaspoon cayenne pepper
1/4 teaspoon ground ginger

or 1/2 teaspoon fine-chopped fresh ginger root
1 clove garlic, chopped fine
4 chicken quarters (any type you like)

1. In a glass, stainless steel, or earthenware baking dish, combine all the ingredients except the chicken. Beat with a fork to mix well. Or, combine the ingredients in a plastic Zip-Loc bag.
2. Place the chicken in the baking dish, rolling each quarter in the marinade. Or place in a plastic bag and shake. Cover and refrigerate for at least 4 hours or overnight, turning the chicken or shaking the plastic bag several times.
3. Remove the chicken from the marinade and place, skin side up, on a baking sheet. Reserve the marinade. Bake in a preheated 350° oven for about an hour, basting with the marinade every 15 minutes and turning the chicken twice.

JAPANESE CUCUMBER SALAD

2 medium cucumbers
3/4 teaspoon salt
3/4 teaspoon sugar
1/4 cup soy sauce
2-1/2 tablespoons vinegar

(preferably rice-wine
vinegar or cider vinegar)
3/4 teaspoon sesame seed oil
(optional)

1. If the cucumbers are waxed, remove the skins. If they are un-
waxed, wash well and dry. Slice cucumbers very thin, then place in a
colander. Toss with the salt and let stand for at least 30 minutes.

2. Gently squeeze excess moisture out of the salted cucumbers
and place them in a serving bowl.

3. In a small bowl or cup, beat together the sugar, soy sauce,
vinegar, and optional sesame oil. Pour over cucumbers and chill until
ready to serve. However, do not combine the cucumbers and dressing
more than a few hours ahead:

A Tuscan Dinner for Fall

Tuscan bean soup (see page 21)

Veal birds with sage butter

Mixed salad

Zabaione (see page 233)

This is one of my favorite dinners and if you work fast, it's one that
can be prepared on short notice, such as when company is coming
only an hour or so after you get home from work. The soup needs
only a few minutes' attention when you use canned beans, but still
tastes long-cooked. The veal birds or rolls can be assembled in about
15 minutes, before guests arrive. They cook about 15 minutes, in the
oven, at the last minute. And zabaione can, in one version, be done
ahead in about 10 minutes or, in the other version, at the last minute
in the same time. In the summer, for an easy, prepare-ahead vegetable

accompaniment, instead of salad, make the baked tomatoes on page 135. Serve the best Chianti *riserva* you can get your hands on. Ruffino Riserva Ducale is a very fine one and is widely available.

VEAL BIRDS WITH SAGE BUTTER

1 pound veal scaloppine, preferably cut from the leg, pounded thin (about 6 cutlets)
Salt and fresh-ground black pepper
1/4 pound prosciutto, sliced paper-thin
1/4 pound sliced bacon, each slice cut in half

12 1/2-inch thick by about 2-inch wide slices Italian bread, preferably day-old
2 small onions, each cut in sixths
1/4 pound (1 stick) butter
2 teaspoons dried leaf sage

1. Cut the slices of veal in half or thirds, depending on their size. You should have 12 pieces about 2-1/2 inches wide and 4 inches long. Arrange all the ingredients, except butter and sage, in front of you. Unless you have a large counter space, you will have to work with only a few piece of veal at a time.

2. Sprinkle the veal lightly with salt and a little more generously with pepper. Place a piece of prosciutto over each slice of seasoned veal, cutting just to cover.

3. Roll up the veal tightly, tucking in the sides. When you have completed 3 veal rolls, start skewering them.

4. On each skewer, place a slice of bread, a wedge of onion, and a veal roll wrapped with a half slice of the bacon. Secure the roll so that the ends of the bacon are held together by the skewer. Repeat with another piece of bread and onion and another veal roll. Repeat again.

5. When all the veal rolls have been skewered, arrange them over a baking dish with the skewers resting on the edges of the dish. Set aside until ready to cook.

6. Meanwhile, in a small saucepan, melt the butter with the sage and let bubble gently for 5 minutes without browning.

7. Just before placing in the oven, baste the skewers with sage butter, making sure to moisten each piece of bread. Cook in a preheated 500° oven for about 6 minutes. Turn the skewers, baste with the remaining butter and whatever drippings are in the pan. Return to the oven and cook another 5 minutes. Baste with fat from the pan and cook another 5 minutes. Serve immediately.

A Dinner Prepared Mostly Ahead

Chicken-liver crostini

Gratinéed veal chops with onion sauce

Watercress and endive salad, mustard-shallot dressing (see page 31)

Mocha-rum mousse (see page 236)

The flavored oil, as well as the garlic toast bases for the chicken-liver crostini or canapés can be prepared well ahead. The livers themselves take only a few minutes to cook, then are mashed right in the skillet. The onion sauce for the chops can be made a few days ahead without sacrifice to flavor; the preliminary searing of the chops and the assembling of the dish, however, should be done the same day you serve them. The assembled chops bake for only 15 minutes. Salad and salad dressing can be prepared ahead and merely tossed together at the last minute. The mousse MUST be prepared ahead.

CHICKEN-LIVER CROSTINI

*12 1/4-inch thick slices
  Italian bread
1 clove garlic, cut in half
4 tablespoons olive oil
1 tiny onion, diced as fine as
  possible
1 clove garlic, chopped fine
1/2 teaspoon dried rosemary,*

*crushed between the
  fingers
3/4 pound chicken livers,
  cleaned
Salt and fresh-ground black
  pepper to taste
1 tablespoon fine-chopped
  parsley*

1. Arrange the bread slices on a baking sheet and place in a pre-heated 300° oven for about 25 minutes or until completely dried. While still hot, rub cut garlic lightly on each slice. (May be prepared ahead and, if made without garlic, kept for several weeks in a tin or wrapped in foil. With garlic, prepare no more than a day ahead.)

2. In a small skillet, heat the oil over medium-low heat and cook the onion, garlic, and rosemary together until rosemary and garlic are lightly browned. (May be prepared ahead.)

3. Ten minutes before serving, heat the flavored oil over medium heat, add the livers and salt and pepper to taste. Cook, stirring frequently, until livers are stiff, but still pink in the center. Remove from heat.

4. With a fork, mash the livers with the oil, until you have a crude paste with some small bits of livers. Check seasoning and mix well.

5. With the fork, mound the liver paste on the bread slices, using the tines of the fork to make the mound neat. Sprinkle with parsley and serve immediately.

GRATINÉED VEAL CHOPS WITH ONION SAUCE

1 teaspoon vegetable oil
4 loin veal chops, 1/2-inch
   thick
2 tablespoons butter
Salt and fresh-ground black
   pepper to taste

1 recipe onion sauce (see
   below)
1-1/2 cups shredded Gruyère
   or Swiss cheese (about 1/4
   pound)

1. In a large skillet, heat the vegetable oil over high heat. Dry the chops with paper toweling, and when the oil is almost smoking, sear them, two at a time, for about 30 seconds on each side or until tinged with brown. As they are done, place in a baking pan or gratin dish greased with 2 tablespoons butter.

2. Season the chops with salt and pepper, then spread the onion sauce over the chops, covering each chop entirely. Sprinkle the shred-

ded cheese over the chops. (May be prepared ahead to this point. Do not refrigerate.)

3. Place in a preheated 375° oven and bake for 12 minutes or until cheese is melted. If necessary, transfer to the broiler and cook another minute or two or until cheese is tinged with brown. Serve within a few minutes.

ONION SAUCE

2 tablespoons butter	1/8 teaspoon fresh-ground
2 pounds onions, sliced thin	black pepper
1 large clove garlic, mashed	Dash nutmeg
3/4 teaspoon salt	1/2 cup heavy cream

1. In a 2-1/2- to 3-quart saucepan, melt the butter over medium heat. Add the onions, garlic, salt, and pepper. Stir to coat with butter, then cover and cook for 1-1/2 hours without browning the onions. Stir occasionally. By the end of the cooking time, onions should be very soft, and some liquid will have accumulated in the pan.

2. Add nutmeg and heavy cream, mix well, then cover again. Cook over medium heat, stirring frequently, until cream has reduced and onions have taken on a pale golden color, about 20 minutes.

3. Remove cover and continue to stir over medium heat another 2 to 3 minutes. Correct seasoning and use to sauce veal, broiled liver, lamb chops, ham, or hamburgers.

A Dinner for Informal Entertaining

Peppers and anchovies
Souvlaki sandwiches on pita bread with chopped salad
Ice cream with honey praline sauce (see page 241)
Strong coffee

The pepper and anchovy appetizer, served at room temperature, calls for bread so that the beautifully flavored oil can be mopped up. Either put the whole casserole on the table and informally dunk into the communal oil well or spoon some extra oil onto each plate. The souvlaki recipe here was inspired by the Greek souvlaki that turn on vertical spits in Greek fast-food restaurants. They call these sandwiches of spitted ground and seasoned meat *gyros,* at least in New York City.

A California red jug wine is appropriate for this unpretentious menu.

PEPPERS AND ANCHOVIES

1 2-ounce can flat anchovy
    fillets
2 pounds green and or red
    peppers, seeded and cut into
    1/2-inch strips

1/2 cup olive oil
4 cloves garlic, crushed or
    chopped fine
1/2 teaspoon fresh-ground
    black pepper

1. In a shallow casserole or baking dish, place the anchovies with their oil. Cut up into small pieces.

2. Add the pepper strips, olive oil, garlic, and black pepper. Toss to mix well and coat the peppers with oil.

3. Cover with foil and bake in a preheated 300° oven for 45 minutes, stirring once or twice.

4. Uncover and cook about 30 minutes longer, stirring once or twice again. Serve at room temperature.

SOUVLAKI

2 pounds twice-ground lamb
    or beef or combination of
    both
2 tablespoons fine-chopped
    parsley
1 large onion, chopped fine
2 to 3 teaspoons dried mint

1 teaspoon oregano
Salt and fresh-ground
    pepper to taste
2 eggs, lightly beaten
1/4 cup (2 ounces) pignoli
    (pine nuts)

1. In a large mixing bowl, combine the meat with parsley and onion. Crumble the mint and oregano between your fingers directly into the bowl. Add salt, pepper, eggs and pignoli. Knead very well.

2. Shape meat into eight rolls about 1-1/2 inches in diameter and about 4 inches long. The rolls can be made longer, if desired, but should be firm and compact at any length. (The souvlaki can be broiled immediately, but will have better flavor if refrigerated overnight.)

3. Broil the rolls, 4 to 5 inches from the heat, for about 15 minutes, turning to brown on all sides.

4. To serve, slice the souvlaki (one 4-inch roll makes one hearty sandwich) and arrange in the pocket of a pita bread. Top with chopped salad without dressing (see page 62). Sauce the sandwich with plain yogurt, sour cream, a mixture of tahini, water, and lemon juice, or a lemon and oil dressing.

Note: Souvlaki can also be served on a plate with boiled rice or a rice pilaf, chopped salad and either plain yogurt or tomato sauce.

Two Formal Dinners for Any Time of Year

Menu A

Cream of mushroom soup (see page 19)
Cornish hens with garlic and liver pâté
Green beans with Parmesan cheese
Mixed green salad
Cheese tray, assorted crackers
Mock mocha mousse (see page 236)

Opinion is divided about Cornish hens. Some people think they are delicious; others find them dry and uninteresting, preferring chicken instead. I must admit I am not among the Cornish hens' biggest fans, but I do like this recipe, and both the hens and this particular preparation make a very nice presentation. The recipe seems long and complicated, but it really isn't. It must be done at the last minute, however. And it does require a blender or food processor. Both the soup and the preliminary cooking of the green beens can be done ahead. And, naturally, the mousse needs to be done ahead. A California Cabernet Sauvignon is appropriate here. Whatever wine you choose, however, make sure there's enough to get through the cheese course.

CORNISH HENS WITH GARLIC AND LIVER PÂTÉ

*4 Cornish hens (with their
  livers)
1/2 lemon
2 tablespoons butter
Salt and fresh-ground
  black pepper
1 tablespoon olive oil
24 unpeeled cloves garlic*

*3/4 pound chicken livers
1/4 cup cognac
Salt and fresh-ground black
  pepper
16 1/2-inch thick slices toasted
  Italian bread
Chopped parsley*

1. Rinse the hens in cold water and pat dry. Rub inside and out with the cut lemon.

2. Massage the outside of each hen with butter, using half a tablespoon of butter for each. Sprinkle lightly all over with salt and pepper.

3. In a casserole just large enough to hold the hens (an 8-quart enameled cast-iron casserole is perfect), heat the olive oil over medium heat. When hot, arrange the hens in the casserole and toss in the unpeeled garlic. Turn the hens until they have a golden glaze all over, in a few minutes.

4. Remove from heat and place 6 cloves of garlic in each of the hens. Replace in casserole.

5. Place in a preheated 375° oven for 5 minutes. Then, with a bulb

baster, baste the hens with the juices and fat in the bottom of the casserole. Return to oven for another 5 minutes.

6. Turn hens, baste again, and continue cooking about 20 minutes, basting one or two more times. Hens are done when their juices run clear when pricked at a joint. They will be lightly browned.

7. While hens are cooking, pick over the hen and chicken livers, cutting off any fat or membranes.

8. When hens are done, remove garlic from cavities and set aside. Allow any juices in the hens to run into the casserole, and place the hens on a serving platter. Cover with foil to keep them warm.

9. Set the casserole over high heat on top of the stove. Add the cognac. Scrape up any browned bits on the bottom of the casserole and let liquid simmer a minute or two.

10. Add the livers and cook about 3 minutes or until they are stiff but still pink inside.

11. Peel the garlic and add 8 cloves to the pulp in the casserole. Discard skins. In a blender or food processor, puree the contents of the casserole.

12. Spread the warm pâté on croutons, sprinkle them with parsley, and surround the hens with liver croutons and the remaining 8 whole cloves garlic. The cooked garlic, 2 cloves per person, can be eaten whole. (Alternately, the pâté can be served in a bowl or crock to be spread on croutons at the table.)

GREEN BEANS WITH PARMESAN CHEESE

Water	4 tablespoons butter
1-1/2 pounds green beans,	Salt
ends broken off and washed	1/2 cup Parmesan cheese

1. Bring a 3-quart saucepan of water to a rolling boil. Add the green beans and boil about 10 minutes or until just tender.

2. Drain well in a colander and run under cold water until green beans are cooled. (May be prepared several hours in advance.)

3. Just before serving, melt the butter over medium-high heat. Add the beans, season with salt to taste, and sauté, stirring almost constantly, until heated through.

4. Add the Parmesan cheese, remove from heat, and mix well. Should be served within a few minutes, although beans do not have to be piping hot.

Menu B

Assorted Appetizers
Risotto with wild mushrooms
Herb-stuffed leg of lamb (see page 125)
Artichokes in garlic butter
Mixed green salad
Stuffed peaches with crema zabaione (see page 233)

If you want to make this dinner an all-out effort you can prepare several antipasti or tapas (Spanish appetizers) yourself; however, you should be able to buy many things at a good Italian delicatessen or in the delicacy department of the supermarket. See Feeding a Crowd for ideas.

Risotto (braised rice) is a first course, not a side dish, and needs to be cooked at the last minute. But it is not difficult to do and worth the time out from your guests that it requires. This risotto is made with imported dried wild mushrooms, which have decidedly more flavor and aroma than cultivated mushrooms. Do not bother making this risotto if you cannot find authentic dried porcini or boletus mushrooms. (They are available in Italian markets and specialty food stores and are not the same as the dried Polish mushrooms often found in supermarkets.) If you follow the recipe leaving out the mushrooms, using all chicken broth, and adding some more cheese than called for, the result will be quite good. For best results Italian Aborio rice should also be used. American long-grain rice will not result in quite the same creamy texture with slightly resistant grains as Italian rice, but the finished dish is still satisfactory.

You should have the lamb boned by the butcher and, if you bring the stuffing along, many butchers will put it in the roast for you before they roll and tie it. The artichokes can be prepared early in the day and require just a final heating before serving. And both the stuffed peaches and zabaione sauce can be done ahead. Serve a refreshing and inexpensive Italian white wine such as Tocai delle Venezie with the antipasti. Gattinara from the Italian Piedmont is perfect for the risotto and main course. A sweet Asti Spumante would be welcome with dessert.

RISOTTO WITH WILD MUSHROOMS

1-1/2 ounces dried porcini or
  boletus mushrooms
3 tablespoons butter
1 tablespoon vegetable oil
1 small onion, chopped very
  fine
2 cups rice (preferably
  Italian Aborio)
1/2 cup dry white wine or
  vermouth

1/2 teaspoon salt
1/4 teaspoon fresh-ground
  black pepper
4 cups (approximately)
  chicken or beef broth
2 tablespoons butter
1/2 cup grated Parmesan
  cheese

1. Crumble the mushrooms into a glass or cup and cover with hot tap water. Let soak at least 20 minutes.

2. Meanwhile, in a 3-quart saucepan, melt the butter with the oil and sauté the onion over medium heat until soft but not browned.

3. Drain the mushrooms, reserving the liquid, and add to the saucepan with the rice. Constantly stir over medium-high heat for about 3 minutes without browning the rice.

4. Add the wine or vermouth, salt, and pepper and stir well. As soon as the liquid is almost evaporated, add enough chicken broth just to cover the rice. Stir again.

5. Simmer steadily, stirring frequently. As soon as the liquid level goes below the rice, add more chicken broth. It should be added gradually so that the rice never stops simmering completely. At some point, add the mushroom liquid instead of chicken broth.

6. The rice should take 18 to 20 minutes to cook from the time the first bit of liquid is added. When finished, it probably will have absorbed a total of about 5 cups of liquid. The mixture should be creamy and fairly loose, but not so loose that it cannot be eaten with a fork. Stir in the butter and cheese and taste for salt and pepper. Serve immediately with extra cheese on the side if desired.

ARTICHOKE HEARTS IN GARLIC BUTTER

2 9-ounce packages frozen
  artichoke hearts, defrosted
6 tablespoons butter

2 large cloves garlic, crushed
Salt and fresh-ground black
  pepper to taste

1. Place a double thickness of paper towel on a baking sheet and drain the artichoke hearts until ready to use.

2. Meanwhile, in a 10- to 12-inch skillet, melt the butter and sauté garlic over medium heat for 2 minutes without browning.

3. Arrange the artichoke hearts in the skillet, in one layer if possible. Season with salt and pepper, cover, and cook over very low heat until artichokes are tender, about 20 minutes. Turn them once during cooking. If not serving immediately, uncover and let cool. Reheat, uncovered, over medium-high heat.

Brunches and Breakfasts

Brunch has become one of the most popular weekend social events, I suppose because it is such a relatively easy way to entertain. It was originally meant to be a cross between breakfast and lunch—a meal taken too late for serving only eggs and a muffin and too early for a heavy multicourse extravaganza. In effect, almost anything goes, and it can be served as early as ten in the morning or as late as one in the afternoon; it can be a light meal or a heavy one.

I do feel, however, that coffee is one constant of brunch and that good coffee, freshly baked rolls, biscuits, or croissants, sweet (unsalted) butter, fresh fruit, and a selection of cheeses and preserves makes a very fine light meal early in the day. Alexis Bespaloff, the wine writer, puts out a large wooden board with a variety of sausage and cheese, loaves of crusty bread, and several mustards and, with a selection of wines to taste, calls it brunch. All these foods are bought at delicatessens and require no preparation whatsoever, but because Bespaloff buys the best, serves it attractively, and invites interesting people, it is always a brunch I look forward to.

There are many recipes throughout this book that can be appropriated for brunch. This chapter, however, presents full menus planned around the inadequacies of a small kitchen. They start with the most breakfast-like meals and end with a buffet menu for a crowd that could just as easily be served for supper.

A Homey Breakfast for Four

Orange Wedges

Baked French Toast

Maple syrup, preserves, honey

Bacon

BAKED FRENCH TOAST

This method of making French toast is not only more delicious than the conventional skillet method: it's more convenient. You can turn out eight slices of hot toast all at once. If you've prepared them the night before and stored them in the refrigerator on a baking sheet, all you have to do is slip them in the oven in the morning.

4 eggs	8 slices firm white bread
1/2 teaspoon salt	2 tablespoons butter
1 cup milk	1/4 cup melted butter

1. In a mixing bowl, beat together the eggs, salt, and milk. Dip bread into egg mixture, turning several times to make sure the bread is thoroughly soaked.

2. Butter a baking sheet with the 2 tablespoons of butter and arrange slices on the sheet. Drizzle melted butter over the bread. (If preparing ahead, cover baking sheet with plastic wrap and refrigerate.)

3. Bake in a preheated 500° oven for 7 to 8 minutes, then turn slices and bake another 4 to 5 minutes or until golden brown. Serve immediately.

A Romantic Breakfast for Two

Baked eggs in cream

Brioche or challah toast

Fresh orange salad with Grand Marnier

This is a light and elegant early morning menu, which can be done with your eyes half closed, perfect for serving to someone in bed.

BAKED EGGS IN CREAM

For each serving: 1 teaspoon Worcestershire sauce
Butter   1 drop Tabasco sauce
1/3 cup heavy cream   2 eggs

1. Butter a small baking dish very generously. Ideally, this should be an individual-serving au gratin dish, but it can be two small custard cups or ramekins, or a coffee cup from a set of ovenproof stoneware.

2. Pour in the cream, Worcestershire sauce, and drop of Tabasco. (If using two small custard cups rather than one large dish, divide the liquids evenly between the two.) Beat with a fork to blend and place in a preheated 500° oven. Bake for about 4 minutes or until cream boils wildly.

3. Remove from oven and immediately turn off oven.

4. Break the eggs into the dish (or one egg into each of two small custard cups) and return to the turned-off oven for 4 to 6 minutes, depending on how firm you wish the yolks to be. Serve immediately.

ORANGE SALAD

3 juice oranges   2 tablespoons orange liqueur

Peel the oranges and slice directly over a bowl to catch all the juice. Add the liqueur. Toss and let stand at room temperature until ready to serve, which can be immediately or not.

A Brunch for Two

Mimosas

Asparagus with "bull's eye" eggs and Parmesan cheese

Cream biscuits

Strawberries in Zinfandel (see page 130)

This is a sensualist's meal because the only way to make the asparagus and egg combination work is to eat the asparagus as you would bread — with your fingers, dip the asparagus into the runny egg yolks and later wipe your plate clean with them. The biscuits, which are really very simple to whip together, can be prepared ahead and baked at the last moment.

ASPARAGUS WITH "BULL'S EYE" EGGS

3/4 pound asparagus
4 tablespoons butter

4 eggs
Fresh-grated Parmesan cheese

1. Break off the tough bottoms of the asparagus, then wash them well under cold water. Bring a skillet of water to a boil, place the asparagus in the skillet and cook until just tender. Exact cooking time depends on size of asparagus, but medium-thickness asparagus should take about 8 minutes. Remove the asparagus with a slotted spoon or skimming spoon and drain on several thickness of paper toweling until ready to serve.

2. In a medium skillet, melt the butter over medium heat. Break the eggs into the skillet and cook over medium heat until whites are set but yolks are still runny.

3. With a spatula, remove the eggs to the two plates you will serve them on and arrange asparagus like spokes with tips at the center of the plate. Be careful not to break yolks.

4. If butter hasn't already begun to brown, increase heat under skillet and cook butter until lightly browned. Pour browned butter over the eggs and asparagus tips and sprinkle grated cheese over all. Serve immediately. Season with salt and pepper at the table.

CREAM BISCUITS

1 cup all-purpose flour
1-1/2 teaspoons baking powder
1/2 teaspoon salt

1/2 tablespoon sugar
1/3 to 1/2 cup heavy cream

1. In a mixing bowl, stir together the flour, baking powder, salt and sugar.

2. Stirring constantly with a fork, mix in cream until dough sticks together. Kneed lightly a few times in the bowl.

3. Drop from a spoon into 6 irregular mounds on a greased baking sheet. (If preparing ahead, cover with plastic and refrigerate.)

4. Bake in the upper third of a preheated 450° oven for 10 to 12 minutes or until golden brown.

MIMOSAS

1 bottle Asti Spumante
1 pint orange juice

2 thin slices orange for garnish
(optional)

Chill both the wine and orange juice very well and mix the two together in a large-stemmed wineglass. A ratio of 6 ounces wine to 3 ounces of juice is usually good. Float a thin slice or half-slice of orange in each glass if desired.

A Summer Brunch for Four

Eggs on anchovy-cheese croutons
Tomato slices with pesto (see page 41)
Baked stuffed peaches (see page 238)

EGGS ON ANCHOVY-CHEESE TOASTS

4 tablespoons butter, at room
  temperature
8 1/2-inch thick slices Italian
  bread
8 anchovy fillets, cut in pieces

1 cup shredded Italian Fontina or
  Bel Paese cheese
3 to 4 tablespoons butter
8 eggs

1. Butter one side of the bread slices. In an 8- to 10-inch skillet, sauté the buttered side of the bread until browned.

2. Arrange bread slices, fried side up, in a lightly greased shallow casserole or baking dish. Place an anchovy fillet on each slice, then cover the slice with shredded cheese. Place casserole in a preheated 350° oven for about 8 minutes or until cheese is bubbly.

3. Meanwhile, in the same skillet, melt butter and quickly fry the eggs four at a time. By the time the first four are done, the cheese should be melted. Place each egg on a toast slice, then proceed to fry remaining eggs. When all the eggs are in place on toast, pour any remaining browned butter from the skillet over the eggs and serve.

A Salad Brunch for Four

Avocados, eggs, and anchovies

Black bread, sweet butter

Tomato slices, scallions, cucumber slices, red radishes

Bloody Marys

AVOCADOS AND EGGS

This can also be served as a first course for an informal dinner, possibly before a substantial soup.

1/3 cup fine-chopped parsley
1 scallion, chopped fine
(including green part)
2 to3 anchovy fillets, chopped
fine
2 cloves garlic, mashed
2 tablespoons wine vinegar
1/2 cup olive oil
Salt and fresh-ground pepper to
taste

2 ripe avocados
1/2 lemon
8 hard-cooked eggs, cut in half
1 cucumber, peeled, if waxed, and
sliced
1 pint cherry tomatoes or 2 large
ripe tomatoes, sliced
8 whole scallions, washed and
trimmed

1. In a small bowl, combine the parsley, scallion, anchovies, and garlic. Stir in the vinegar, then beat in the olive oil. Season to taste and set aside.

2. Cut avocados in half and rub on lemon to prevent discoloration. Remove pit, peel, and cut into crescent slices.

3. On one large or four individual plates, arrange avocado slices with the egg halves. Beat the dressing again, pour over eggs and avocados, and garnish with cucumber slices, cherry tomatoes, or sliced tomatoes and whole scallions.

Variation: Devotees of anchovies may want to garnish each serving with extra whole anchovy fillets. A few olives wouldn't be out of place either.

BLOODY MARYS

Bloody Marys have become the standard brunch cocktail. There is even a myth that they cure hangovers. They are not my favorite drink, but they are a big improvement over plain tomato juice and work beautifully in this menu.

1 quart tomato juice
5 teaspoons Worcestershire sauce
3 or 4 tablespoons lemon juice
1 teaspoon celery salt

1-1/2 cups vodka
Tabasco to taste
Lemon or lime wedges, seeded

Stir all the ingredients together in a pitcher and chill well. Serve in stemmed or highball glasses, on ice if desired. Garnish with lemon or lime.

An Expensive Brunch for Six

Seafood strata
Endive and watercress salad with mustard-shallot dressing
Melon balls with rum and brown sugar (see page 243)
California Chardonnay

SEAFOOD STRATA

It is inconvenient, if not impossible, to make pastry in a small kitchen, but you can still serve a quichelike dish for brunch without resorting to frozen pie shells. A strata is a sort of savory bread-and-butter pudding with a custard texture. This one is filled with seafood as well as cheese, and I think it is better than most quiche that is served these days.

1 tablespoon butter
6 slices firm-type white bread
3 tablespoons butter
1/2 pound cooked crabmeat, flaked, or 1/2 pound shrimp, chopped (or a combination of both)
1 rib celery, chopped fine
1 tiny onion, chopped fine
1/3 cup mayonnaise
2 cups shredded Gruyère or

Swiss cheese (or a mixture, including some Parmesan cheese)
6 slices firm-type white bread
3 tablespoons butter
4 eggs
2 cups milk or half-and-half
1 teaspoon Dijon mustard
1/4 teaspoon fresh-ground black pepper

1. With the first tablespoon of butter, grease an 11 3/4- by 7 1/2-inch baking or gratin dish, or one of about equivalent size.

2. Trim six slices of bread to fit the bottom of the dish. Butter the top side of each slice with 1/2 tablespoon of butter. Place, buttered side up, in the dish.

3. In a mixing bowl, combine the crabmeat and/or shrimp, celery, onion, and mayonnaise. With a fork, mix well.

4. Spread the seafood mixture evenly over the bread in the dish. Scatter the cheese evenly over the seafood.

5. Trim the other six slices of bread. Butter them on one side. Place them in the dish buttered side down.

6. In a mixing bowl, beat together the eggs, milk or half-and-half, mustard, and pepper. Pour evenly over the casserole, cover with plastic, and refrigerate for at least 2 hours or until ready to bake, which can be the next day.

7. Bake in a preheated 350° oven for 35 to 40 minutes or until puffed and browned lightly. Let cool 10 minutes before slicing and serving.

A Basque Brunch for Four

Piperade

Slices of prosciutto or ham   Toasted whole grain bread

Green salad with walnuts

Rioja Sangria

PIPERADE

Piperade, a Basque amalgam of peppers, tomatoes, onions, and eggs, is to me a minor feast because the word immediately conjures up the flavors of smoky Bayonne ham and toasted coarse-grained bread, its usual accompaniments.

Unfortunately, Bayonne ham is nearly unobtainable and outrageously expensive when it is. Italian prosciutto, although it is unlike the French Bayonne, is a decent alternative. Better still, though, is to plan on making piperade soon after you've braised your own ham in Madeira (see page 195). There are few better ways to finish off the leftovers than with a dish of piperade.

Like ratatouille, its Provençal cousin, piperade is best when made with fresh tomatoes in season. However, imported canned plum tomatoes are a satisfactory enough substitute and much better than fresh tomatoes when they are not vine-ripened.

The piperade base without eggs, also like ratatouille, can be made ahead, stored in the refrigerator for a number of days, and can be used to fill crepes, as a side dish for broiled or roasted chicken, lamb, or beef or a base on which to bake fish fillets or a fish steak (See ratatouille, page 158).

5 tablespoons olive oil, combination butter and olive oil, or rendered preservative-free bacon fat
1 pound onions, sliced very thin
1 pound green and/or red peppers, seeded and cut into 1/2-inch strips

1 pound fresh plum tomatoes, seeded and chopped or 1 1-pound can imported plum tomatoes, drained and chopped
Salt and fresh-ground black pepper to taste
3/4 teaspoon dried marjoram
8 eggs

1. In a 10- to 12-inch skillet, heat whichever fat you are using. Add onions and sauté over medium heat until golden but not browned, about 20 minutes.

2. Add the peppers, cover and cook for 10 minutes or until peppers are wilted.

3. Add tomatoes, season with salt, pepper, and marjoram, cover partially and simmer for 15 to 20 minutes or until tomatoes become saucey. The peppers will be quite soft, but still hold their shape. (May be prepared ahead to this point and, when cooled to room temperature, stored in the refrigerator for a week or so. When ready to serve, reheat in the same skillet before continuing with recipe.)

4. In a large bowl, beat eggs very well, then pour them over the hot, but not quite simmering, vegetable mixture. Cook the eggs very slowly until set but still creamy, occasionally scraping them up from the bottom with a spatula. Serve immediately.

Variations: Instead of beating the eggs and scrambling them with the vegetables, pour the vegetable mixture into a well-greased baking dish. Break the eggs over the top and bake in a preheated 350° oven until eggs have set to desired degree, usually 10 to 12 minutes.

Or, carefully break eggs into skillet with vegetables and do not mix. Cover and cook over medium heat until eggs are poached to desired degree, usually about 5 minutes.

Or, heat the piperade to a simmer and serve with bull's eye or once-over eggs on top.

RIOJA SANGRIA

1 bottle Rioja wine	1 cup carbonated water
Juice of 2 oranges	1 orange, cut in wedges
Juice of 1 lemon	1 apple, cut in chunks
1/2 cup brandy	

With a wooden spoon, stir the wine, fruit juices, brandy, and water together in a large pitcher. Add the fruit and enough ice to fill the pitcher. Serve in stemmed glasses. Leave the spoon in the pitcher to retrieve the pieces of fruit.

A Brunch for Four for Winter Afternoons

Monte Cristo sandwiches

New England baked beans

Fresh fruit

Riesling wine

MONTE CRISTO SANDWICHES

8 slices firm white bread
4 tablespoons butter, at room
  temperature
8 slices baked Virginia ham
8 slices Switzerland Swiss or
  Gruyère cheese

4 slices turkey breast
5 eggs
1/2 teaspoon salt
3 tablespoons butter

1. To make each sandwich, butter two slices of bread on one side only with about 1/2 tablespoon of butter.

2. On the buttered side of one slice, place a slice of ham, a slice of cheese, a slice of turkey, another slice of cheese, then another slice of ham. Place the other buttered slice of bread, buttered side down, on top.

3. In a deep dish or bowl, beat the eggs well with the salt and 3 tablespoons of water. Dip each sandwich in the egg, turning several times to make sure each sandwich is well soaked. Set dipped sandwiches on a plate until ready to cook. (If preparing them more than an hour or so ahead, cover with plastic and refrigerate.)

4. In a skillet, heat the remaining butter and fry sandwiches until golden brown on both sides.

NEW ENGLAND BAKED BEANS

As far as food and wine combinations go, it is hard to beat the pairing of New England baked beans and a slightly sweet Riesling wine. Although they are worlds apart in origin, they enhance each other's flavors. Of course, I am inordinately fond of baked beans and a little partial to the Riesling grape.

1 pound small white beans (pea
  beans)
6 cups cold water
1/2 pound salt pork (as lean as
  possible)
1 small onion

2 whole cloves
2 teaspoons salt
1 teaspoon dry mustard
1/3 cup brown sugar
1/4 cup molasses

1. Pick through the beans, then rinse under cold running water. In a 3-quart saucepan, combine the beans and water. Bring to a boil, cover and simmer gently for 1 to 1-1/2 hours or until beans are just tender.

2. Drain beans, reserving the liquid in a large bowl.

3. Cut half the salt pork into thin slices and arrange the slices on the bottom of a 2-quart casserole or bean pot. Cover with half the beans. Stud the onion with the cloves and half bury it in the beans.

4. Add the remaining beans. Score the remaining piece of salt pork down to the rind and place on top.

5. Measure out 2 cups of the reserved bean liquid and stir in the salt, mustard, brown sugar, and molasses. Pour over the beans. Cover and bake in a preheated 300° oven for 5 to 7 hours, stirring occasionally and adding more bean liquid to keep the beans moist. Can be prepared ahead and reheated.

An Afternoon Italian Brunch for Six

Sformata di salami

Green salad   Carlo's Mushroom Salad (see page 63)

Crusty bread

Fresh fruit   Amaretti di Saronno

SFORMATA DI SALAME

Sformate are generally made with vegetables and served as a separate but secondary course, sometimes with a sauce. However, this sformata, studded with cubes of Genoa salami and filled with cheese, is both an impressive and suitable main course for brunch.

1/2 cup butter
3/4 cup all-purpose flour
1-1/2 cups milk
1/8 teaspoon nutmeg
1 teaspoon salt
1/4 teaspoon fresh-ground black
   pepper

3 ounces grated Parmesan cheese
   (about 1 cup)
4 ounces grated Fontina or Gruyère cheese (about 1-1/2 cups)
8 ounces Genoa salami in one
   piece, cut into 1/4-inch cubes
4 eggs

1. Use 2 tablespoons of the butter to liberally grease a 9-by-5 loaf pan. Sprinkle the inside of the pan with 2 tablespoons of the grated Parmesan cheese and set aside.

2. In a 2- to 3-quart saucepan, melt the remaining butter over medium heat, then blend in the flour with a wooden spoon or wire whisk. Let cook, without coloring, for about 3 minutes. Remove from heat and allow bubbling to subside.

3. Stirring vigorously and constantly, add the milk and replace over medium-low heat. Continue to stir constantly until smooth and thickened. Remove from heat.

4. Stir in the nutmeg, salt, pepper, both cheeses, and the salami. Beat in the eggs one at a time, making sure they are well incorporated.

5. Pour into the prepared loaf pan and bake in a preheated 350° oven for about 1 hour and 10 minutes or until puffed and browned. Let cool 10 minutes, unmold on a serving plate, and cut into slices.

A Fill-Your-Own Crepe Buffet

Chicken curry   Ratatouille (see page 158)

Strawberries in two Liqueurs (see page 242)

Cream cheese and nut filling (see page 244)

Red and white wine   Beer

The idea is not to have any work to do once your guests arrive. The crepes can be prepared ahead (see page 244), wrapped in foil and frozen, then heated through in their foil envelopes. Wrap them in a large napkin to keep them warm and serve them in a decorative basket. Chicken curry can be made ahead and gently reheated. Serve it in a chafing dish or earthenware casserole placed over an alcohol lamp. The ratatouille can be prepared ahead also, but serve it at room temperature. Do not freeze the cream cheese and nut filling; refrigerate it and remember to remove it well before it's served to give it time to soften. The strawberries do have to be prepared the same morning as the brunch. Bury the white wine and beer halfway in a large bed of ice — I use my aluminum stockpot with copper handles or large enameled casserole for this — put out plates, forks, and glasses, and let your guests roll their own crepes.

CHICKEN CURRY

6 tablespoons butter
3 medium onions, chopped
2 tablespoons curry powder
4 tablespoons flour
2 cups chicken broth
1 cup milk

3 pounds chicken breast cutlets,
   cut into 1-inch cubes
1 10-ounce box frozen tiny peas,
   (petit pois) defrosted
2 green apples, peeled, cored, and
   cubed

1. In a deep 12-inch skillet, melt the butter over medium heat and sauté onions until tender but not browned.

2. Blend in the curry powder and flour and continue to sauté for about 4 minutes. Remove from heat and allow bubbling to subside.

3. Stir in the chicken broth and milk. Return skillet to high heat and, stirring constantly, bring to a simmer. Sauce should be thickened and smooth.

4. Add the chicken and peas and apples. Stir well, then return to simmer. Simmer very gently for 5 to 10 minutes or until chicken is cooked tender. *Makes 10 to 12 servings.*

A Brunch Buffet for Twelve

Braised ham in Madeira

Chicken salad (see below)

Cold asparagus vinaigrette

Cream biscuits (see page 183)

Fresh cottage cheese   Pickled watermelon rind   Preserves

Rosé wine

Ham is a classic buffet item and perfect for brunch. This one is braised in an aromatic Madeira bouillon in a large casserole on top of the stove or in the oven. Even a small ham of about 8 pounds will feed more than 12 on this menu, so you will have plenty of leftovers to make the jambalaya on page 76 or to eat with piperade, page 187.

A nice chicken salad for this menu would be one with tarragon-flavored mayonnaise and sliced almonds, and the asparagus can be served with lemon juice and oil dressing instead of a vinegar dressing.

The adjective *fresh* for cottage cheese is very important, because cottage cheese that is more than a few days old is simply not worth eating unless one is forced to by reason of obesity. In some parts of the country, it is possible to buy fresh and very creamy cottage cheese in bulk. To me, when cottage cheese is good, it is very good and doesn't taste a bit like diet food.

HAM BRAISED IN MADEIRA

1 carrot
1 onion
1 bay leaf
2 cups dry Madeira wine
1 cup beef broth or bouillon

15 peppercorns
1 8- to 9-pound fully cooked
   ham (not canned)
Maple syrup (optional)

1. In any pot you can get the ham into comfortably, combine all the ingredients except the ham and the maple syrup. Cover, bring to a boil and boil for 15 minutes.

2. Meanwhile, cut off any skin or excess fat from the ham. However, you should leave a thin layer of fat.

3. Place the ham in the pot, cover, and simmer very gently for 1-1/2 hours or until the bone is slightly loose. Baste the ham about every 15 minutes.

4. Remove from heat and allow to cool in the broth. Clean the surface of the ham with a paper towel.

5. If you wish to glaze the ham, place in a roasting pan, spoon on some maple syrup and place in a preheated 400° oven. In 3 minutes, baste with more maple syrup and then again 3 or 4 minutes later.

Feeding a Crowd:
Party Food

No matter what size kitchen you have, feeding more than a few people is always something of a chore. Even when simple dishes are prepared in quantities for eight and more, the sheer volume of food can create havoc in a small kitchen. High-gear organization obviously becomes a necessity.

A cheese-and-wine party is painless to arrange and the least taxing on your kitchen. But, frankly, unless it is planned as a tasting of interesting or related wines paired with a few out-of-the-ordinary cheeses, it can be pretty boring to the palate. There are other ready-to-eat foods which you might add if quality versions are available in your area. Among them are all kinds of European-style cold cuts, American country ham, jarred and delicatessen-pickled vegetables, smoked fish, and various kinds of jarred and delicatessen herring. I prefer to stay away from pretzels and potato chips and I like nuts and flavorful imported olives. The canned olives from California are too bland for my taste.

Although on a philosophical level I hate the idea of making lists, they are the only practical way to organize a party even if you are only assembling store-bought food. Besides a detailed shopping list prepared at least a week ahead, you should have a list of the food you will be serving and any garnishes and a third list with all the serving plates and bowls you will need and what food goes on them. As a guide and reminder, post these lists on the refrigerator door with a magnet. Copy any recipes onto small pieces of paper. The writing forces you to review the recipe, and once it is on a slip of paper you can stick it on the refrigerator as a guide. If you buy all imperishables well ahead of time, cook things ahead whenever possible and set up a self-service bar, there's no reason you can't enjoy your own party.

Home bar service today has become much easier and more acceptably informal now that almost everyone drinks wine. It's still gracious to put out a few bottles of spirits—at least one brown goods such as scotch or bourbon and one white goods such as vodka or gin—a bucket of ice, soda, tonic, and lemon and lime wedges. But just a choice of white wine or red wine seems to be acceptable in many circles. One bottle of wine for every two to three guests is a rough rule of thumb for a party lasting several hours. Red wine should be served at cool room temperature, white wine chilled. So I don't have continually to run to the refrigerator to replenish cold white wine, I open several bottles at once and put them on ice in either a particularly attractive stockpot or large enameled cast-iron casserole, depending on the number of bottles that have to be kept cold.

Raw Vegetables and Dips

Raw vegetables, or crudités, as the French call them, are dependable, attractive, and easy to prepare as a snack to go with drinks. Most of the time you'll want to serve an assortment carefully arranged in a serving bowl. But sometimes it is effective to serve just one vegetable. When asparagus are in season, for instance, snap off the tough ends, wash them and arrange the raw stalks standing up in a vase or clay flowerpot and serve with the garlic dip given below.

Red radishes arranged in a bowl with ice can be served with cold sweet (unsalted) butter and coarse salt to dab on them.

Serve cherry tomatoes surrounded with three bowls—one filled with vodka or gin, one with curry powder, and one with coarse salt. I believe this is a James Beard invention. At least I know he's served this at parties and everyone has enjoyed dipping the tomatoes into all the bowls.

Raw mushrooms are attractive in a napkin-lined basket and delicious in the garlic dip below.

GARLIC DIP

This has a homemade olive oil mayonnaise base into which sour cream is blended. Parsley and chives give an attractive green color. Lemon juice, capers, and garlic add a delicious bite.

1 egg
Heaping 1/4 teaspoon Dijon
  mustard
1/4 teaspoon salt
1 tablespoon lemon juice
1/2 cup chopped parsley
  (tightly packed)

2 cloves garlic, chopped
  coarse
2 tablespoons capers
1/4 cup chopped chives
1 cup olive oil
1 tablespoon lemon juice
1 cup sour cream

1. In a blender or food processor, combine the egg, mustard, salt, and lemon juice. Process briefly to just blend. Add the parsley, garlic, capers, and chives. Process briefly again.

2. Put the machine on and gradually add the olive oil. When all has been added, the mixture should be a medium-bodied mayonnaise.

3. Pour the mayonnaise into a mixing bowl and stir in the remaining lemon juice and the sour cream. Correct seasoning if necessary and chill well before serving. *Makes about 2-1/2 cups.*

ROZANNE GOLD'S GREEN PEPPERCORN SAUCE

Ms. Gold, who used to cook for Mayor Edward Koch of New York, uses this sauce with roast shells of beef. It is equally good as a vegetable dip.

1-1/2 cups mayonnaise
1 cup sour cream
1/4 cup Dijon mustard
1/4 cup grainy Pommery
  mustard

1 small can green Madagascar
  peppercorns

1. In a mixing bowl, beat together the mayonnaise, sour cream, and two mustards.

2. Drain the peppercorns, reserving the liquid, and stir the peppercorns into the sauce. Stir in a little of the reserved liquid to taste. Cover and refrigerate for 24 hours before serving. *Makes 3 cupfuls.*

Two Blender or Food Processor Pâté Spreads

Both these recipes are very simple to prepare if you have a blender or food processor. The first is possible to make in a meat grinder or by hand in a wooden chopping bowl with a curved-bladed chopper, but a machine is essential for making the second pâté very smooth.

COARSE PORK AND CHICKEN LIVER PÂTÉ

This is a fairly rustic spread.

3 to 4 tablespoons butter
2 medium onions, chopped
   fine
1 pound sweet Italian sausage
   meat, removed from casings
1 pound chicken livers
1/2 teaspoon nutmeg
1/4 teaspoon allspice

1 tablespoon cognac
1 tablespoon Madeira
1 tablespoon fine-chopped
   parsley
Salt and fresh-ground
   pepper to taste (if
   necessary)

1. In an 8- to 10-inch skillet, heat the butter and sauté onions over medium heat until tender but not browned.

2. Add the sausage meat and cook until it has lost its raw color.

3. Add the chicken livers and cook until firm but still slightly pink inside.

4. Using a slotted spoon, put a small amount of the mixture into a blender. Process on low speed until mostly pureed, but still containing a few coarse pieces. Scrape into a mixing bowl and repeat until all

of mixture is pureed. (If using a food processor, you can process about half the mixture at a time.)

5. Add the nutmeg, allspice, cognac, Madeira, and parsley to the bowl with the puree. With a wooden spoon, beat very well. Taste and correct seasoning, if necessary.

6. Pack into a crock or serving bowl, if desired, and chill. Pâté will improve if left to age for 24 hours. Serve with bread and/or plain crackers. *Makes about 8 servings.*

Variation: Instead of serving pâté as a spread, pack it into a hollowed-out loaf of French bread which you can later slice. Split the bread in half the long way, leaving one side of the crust intact to make a hinge. Pull out excess dough from the center. If desired, spread lightly with softened butter. Fill up the cavity in the bread so that when it is closed the pâté will completely fill it. Wrap in aluminum foil and chill several hours until pâté is firm enough to be sliced. *Makes enough to fill one 24-inch loaf of French bread. 8 to 10 servings.*

SMOOTH CHICKEN-LIVER PÂTÉ

Elegantly smooth. I have seen similar pâtés served in baroque curls formed by a heated silver spoon used to dig out each serving from an enormous crock—an impressive show.

1 pound chicken livers, chopped coarse	1/2 teaspoon salt
1 small onion, chopped fine	Large pinch ground allspice
2 tablespoons butter	1/4 teaspoon fresh-ground black pepper
1/4 cup cognac	Large pinch dried thyme
1/3 cup heavy cream	4 tablespoons melted butter

1. In an 8- to 10-inch skillet, sauté the livers and onion in the 2 tablespoons of butter until the livers are firm, but still slightly pink inside.

2. Place the livers and onion in the jar of a blender or food processor.

3. Add the cognac to the skillet and reduce to a few tablespoons while scraping up any bits left by the livers. With a rubber spatula, scrape the liquid into the blender.

4. Add the cream and seasonings and process until it is a smooth paste. In a blender, it may be necessary to turn the machine on and off to scrape and mix the contents down toward the blades.

5. Pour in the melted butter and process until perfectly smooth and well blended.

6. Taste carefully for seasoning, then pack into a crock or serving bowl. Chill well — pâté will improve if left to age for 24 hours — but remove from refrigerator about 45 minutes before serving. Serve with bread or plain crackers. *Makes about 6 to 8 servings.*

HUMMUS

Few dips or spreads are as addictive as hummus. No matter how much I make, my guests always wipe the plate clean. This recipe was given to me by an Israeli woman, although hummus is popular all over the Middle East. She, like me, has a penchant for garlic, but you may certainly decrease the amount to taste. This is another one of those very adjustable dishes, and after you've made it once or twice you'll end up devising a personal formula. By the way, many recipes for hummus incorporate olive oil in the dip as well as using it as a sort of garnish. Leaving out the oil, however, doesn't seem to harm the flavor and makes the dip a lot less caloric. Tahina (sesame paste) is now available at most health food stores.

2 20-ounce or 3 16-ounce cans chick-peas, drained (reserve at least 1 cup of liquid)	*6 to 8 cloves garlic, mashed*
	1 tablespoon salt
	Paprika
1 pound tahina (sesame paste)	*Olive oil*
	Fine-chopped parsley
Juice of 4 or 5 lemons	*Oil-cured or Greek olives*

1. In a blender or food processor, in several batches, puree the chick-peas with the tahina, lemon juice, and garlic. Use up to 1 cup of the reserved chick-pea liquid to make pureeing easier. This will not be needed in a food processor, but you may want to add it anyway to make a less pasty hummus. The extra liquid will, however, most certainly be needed in a blender.

2. Stir in the salt and spread the hummus on a large platter. Using a spoon or spatula, shape the hummus so it is heaped slightly in the middle and around the edges of the platter with a sort of valley between.

3. Sprinkle paprika on the center mound, then drizzle a few tablespoons of olive oil over the paprika. The paprika will run slightly and the oil will end up in the valley. Sprinkle parsley around the edge of the platter and, if desired, space olives around the edge. *Makes about 10 servings.*

BABA GANOUSH

The only difference between hummus and baba ganoush is that the first is made with chick-peas and the second with eggplant. Tahina, lemon juice, garlic, and garnishes remain the same. The following recipe makes a large amount, but exactly how many it will serve is hard to say. Everyone I know is just as wild about baba ganoush as they are about hummus.

5 pounds eggplant	3 cloves garlic, crushed
3/4 pound tahina (sesame paste)	1/3 cup olive oil
	Salt to taste
Juice of 3 lemons	Olive oil

1. Wash the eggplants, then place whole on a baking sheet. Bake in a preheated 350° oven for about 45 minutes or until very tender. Exact cooking time will depend on freshness and size of eggplants.

(A much messier and more tedious way to cook the eggplants, albeit a more authentic and tasty way, is to impale each eggplant on a fork and roast it over a gas burner until tender.)

2. Cut the eggplants open and let them drain in a bowl until cool enough to handle. Pour off the liquid that accumulates in the bowl.

3. Working with your hands and a small, sharp knife, cut the eggplant flesh away from the skins. Discard the skins.

4. Using a potato masher or food processor, mash or chop the eggplant until fine, but not pureed. If you have used a food processor, return the eggplant to the bowl.

5. Add the tahina, lemon juice, garlic, oil, and salt. Mix very well. Correct seasoning and mix again. Chill before serving, but do not serve very cold. *Makes about 10 servings.*

EGGPLANT SALAD

As in the previous two recipes, take the proportions here loosely and develop the balance of flavors to your own taste.

3 large eggplants	*Salt and fresh-ground pepper*
1 medium onion	*to taste*
2 large cloves garlic, crushed	*Paprika*
or chopped very fine	*Fine-chopped parsley*
1/2 cup olive oil	*Oil-cured or Greek olives*

1. Wash the eggplants and place them on a baking sheet. Bake in a preheated 350° oven until eggplants have totally collapsed.

2. Using a pot holder or towel to hold the hot eggplant over a mixing bowl by the stem end, cut open the large ends. Lean the eggplants open-end-down against the side of the bowl and let them drain until cooled. Pour off and discard the liquid in the bowl.

3. Peel the eggplants over the bowl (it is a messy job) and discard the skins. (If by some chance you can get the flesh out without tearing the skins, you can pile the salad in them for serving.)

4. Grate the onion into the bowl. Add the garlic. With a fork or potato masher, mash the eggplant as fine as possible. A blender or food processor can also be used for this.

5. Beat in the olive oil and season with salt and pepper. Chill until ready to serve. The salad is best made a day ahead. Beat again before serving. Garnish with chopped parsley, black olives, or a sprinkling of paprika. *Makes about 8 servings.*

GUACAMOLE

Almost everyone loves guacamole and it is very easy to prepare all in one bowl.

2 tablespoons fine-chopped fresh (or canned) green chili peppers or more to taste
1 small onion, chopped very fine

1 medium ripe tomato, diced fine
2 medium ripe avocados
1/2 teaspoon salt (or to taste)

1. In a mixing bowl, combine the peppers, onion, and tomato.

2. Peel the avocados. Remove and reserve the pits. Cut the avocado pulp into the bowl, season with salt, then mash coarsely with a fork. Mix well.

3. Embed the avocado pits in the guacamole to retard discoloration. Refrigerate until ready to serve. Do not hold for more than a few hours. Remove pits before serving. *Makes about 3 cups.*

GUACAMOLE TOSTADOS

Once you've made guacamole, it's an easy step to these tostados, a more substantial snack. In many parts of the country you can buy excellent packaged fresh tortillas in the supermarket, and frozen tortillas are even more widely available.

Oil for frying
12 fresh or frozen tortillas
1/2 pound Jack or milk
    cheddar cheese, shredded
3 cups guacamole (see
    preceding recipe)

1 cup sour cream
2 cups fine-shredded romaine
    lettuce
Canned peeled green chili
    peppers to taste, seeded and
    cut into strips

1. In a skillet, heat 1/2 inch of oil until it just begins to smoke. Turn heat down, but keep oil very hot.

2. Fry the tortillas one or two at a time without overlapping. Fry until edges are crisp but center is still slightly soft. As the tortillas are done, place on a paper-lined baking sheet to drain.

3. Remove the paper from the baking sheet and sprinkle cheese over the tostados (fried tortillas). Place in a preheated 350° oven until cheese is melted.

4. Spread guacamole over each tostado, spoon on a dollop of sour cream, sprinkle with shredded lettuce, and garnish with pepper strips. *Makes 6 servings.*

TIPSY EDAM

A cheese spread, this is best made in a food processor or blender, but it can also be done by hand. Grind the nuts in a rotary nut and cheese grater.

1 baby Edam cheese
    (9 ounces)
1 3-ounce package cream
    cheese

2 tablespoons bourbon or
    cognac (approximately)
1/4 cup ground pecans
1 tablespoon grated onion

1. Cut off the top third of the cheese. With a sharp knife or a melon baller, scoop out the cheese from the large portion, leaving about 1/8 inch of cheese as a supporting wall. Place the cheese in a mixing bowl and cut it up as small as possible. (If you are using a food processor, the pieces don't have to be very small.)

2. Remove the red wax covering from the smaller portion and cut up that cheese.

3. Add the remaining ingredients and, with a fork, mash together until well blended. Or put all the ingredients in a food processor or blender and process into a paste. Add a little more spirits if necessary to make mixture more spreadable.

4. Spoon the mixture back into the Edam case and smooth the mounded top. Cover with plastic and refrigerate until ready to serve. The spread is best made a day ahead, and it will keep for a week or more if carefully covered. *Makes 8 servings.*

LIPTAUER CHEESE SPREAD

1/2 pound sweet (unsalted) butter
1 8-ounce package cream cheese
2 tablespoons mashed anchovies or anchovy paste
2 tablespoons sweet Hungarian paprika
1 teaspoon caraway seed
2 tablespoons Dijon mustard
1 small onion, chopped fine

1. Place butter and cream cheese in mixing bowl and allow to come to room temperature.

2. With the back of a spoon, blend them together with the remaining ingredients until evenly colored. Refrigerate until 15 minutes before serving. Can be kept refrigerated for several days. Serve with crackers, black bread, or whole-grain flat bread. Or use to stuff celery.

BLUE CHEESE AND APPLE CANAPÉS

These can be prepared for the oven ahead of time and are an interesting marriage of flavors.

For each serving assemble:
1 tablespoon butter
3 1/4-inch thick slices
  Italian bread

1/2 medium apple, cored
1-1/2 to 2 ounces blue cheese

1. Butter each slice of bread on one side. Arrange the bread, buttered side down, on a baking sheet and bake in a preheated 375° oven until the top side is toasted and bottom browned. Remove from the oven and turn over all the bread slices.

2. On each slice of bread place a slice of apple, then crumble cheese on top of the apple. Set aside until ready to serve.

3. Before serving, place the canapés under the broiler (you may have to take them off the baking sheet) for less than a minute, just until the cheese melts. Serve immediately.

MARINATED MUSHROOMS

These are handy to have on hand in the refrigerator for drop-in guests. They will keep for several weeks before they become too strongly flavored. When they are all eaten you can re-use the marinade to make a fresh batch.

2 cups water
1 cup olive oil
1/2 cup wine vinegar
1/2 teaspoon fennel seed
1 large bay leaf

12 whole peppercorns
2 teaspoons salt
1/2 teaspoon tarragon
4 whole sprigs parsley
1 pound mushrooms

1. In a 3-quart saucepan, combine all the ingredients except mushrooms. Bring to a boil, cover, and boil for 10 minutes.

2. If mushrooms are small, leave them whole. Otherwise cut them in halves or quarters. Add them to the marinade and boil 10 to 15 minutes or until mushrooms are dark through the center. Let cool in marinade, then pour all into jars. Refrigerate until ready to serve.

Tapas

In Spain, especially in Andalucia, tapas are virtually a way of life. Although they are what we might call appetizers, at least judging them on size of portion, they are not necessarily consumed before a meal the way Italian antipasti or French hors d'oeuvres usually are. They are eaten for their own sake with generally copious amounts of fino sherry, the driest type. The following four recipes are all tapas and you might want to serve them with chilled *fino* sherry straight up the way the Spaniards do.

TORTILLA ESPAÑOLA
(SPANISH OMELET)

This is the true Spanish omelet, served there in wedges or squares. To make a really good Spanish omelet you will have to use fruity olive oil and two skillets. I've found that it's difficult to get the potatoes and onions to cook properly if you do them in a skillet that's small enough to make a thick, moist omelet. And if you make the omelet in a skillet big enough to cook the vegetables easily, the omelet is too thin. The little extra effort of using two skillets is definitely worthwhile, but if you must, use just the smaller one. Although the omelet is most usually served at room temperature, the fresher it is, the better. It should not be made more than several hours before serving.

4 tablespoons olive oil	1/2 teaspoon salt
1 pound potatoes, peeled and cut into 1/2-inch cubes	5 or 6 eggs
	Salt to taste
1/2 pound onions, chopped fine	Fresh-ground black pepper to taste (optional)

1. In an 8- to 10-inch skillet, heat the oil over medium heat. Add the potatoes and onions and immediately reduce heat to low. Sprinkle

with salt and mix well. Sauté the potatoes and onions slowly, shaking the pan frequently to prevent sticking, and tossing the mixture occasionally, until onions are almost a puree and the potatoes are very tender. Neither vegetable should brown.

2. Meanwhile, in a mixing bowl, beat the eggs well.

3. When vegetables are done, remove from heat. Let the vegetables cool a few minutes.

4. With a slotted spoon, remove the vegetables, leaving behind as much of the oil as possible. Place vegetables in bowl with eggs and mix well, seasoning with salt and optional pepper to taste.

5. Drain the fat from the large skillet into a smaller skillet (5 to 7 inches). Heat oil over medium heat, pour in the egg mixture, and immediately reduce heat to low. Cook omelet until all but the top of the omelet is set and the bottom is only very lightly browned, 5 to 8 minutes.

6. Slide the omelet, cooked side down, onto a plate. Turn the skillet over the omelet on the plate. Then, flip the omelet and skillet over so it is now uncooked side down in the skillet. Return skillet to low heat and continue to cook another minute or so or until the second side is just set. It should not be browned at all. Flip the omelet onto a serving plate, second side up. Cool to room temperature before slicing and serving. Cut into wedges or cubes. *Makes about 6 appetizer servings.*

MUSHROOMS SAUTÉED WITH GARLIC AND HOT PEPPER

These mushrooms sound so simple, you wouldn't think they'd be as delicious as they are. Serve them with toothpicks to handle them and plenty of dry sherry to wash them down. They need to be made at the last minute, but take only a few minutes to cook.

4 tablespoons olive oil
5 to 6 whole peeled garlic
  cloves
2 whole dried chili peppers

1 pound small mushrooms
  (cut large ones in halves or
  quarters)
Salt to taste

1. In a large skillet, combine the oil, garlic, and peppers. Place over medium-low heat and sauté until garlic is lightly browned on all sides. (May be prepared ahead.)

2. Raise heat to medium high and add the mushrooms. Tossing constantly, sauté the mushrooms for about 3 minutes or until just done. Season to taste with salt and serve immediately. *Makes about 6 appetizer servings.*

DEVILED NUTS

Serve these as part of a tapas array or anytime you need something for people to nibble with drinks. They are better and less expensive than any similar store-bought nuts.

1 pound shelled walnuts,
  pecans, or filberts
  (hazelnuts)
1/3 cup butter
1 teaspoon Worcestershire sauce

1/2 teaspoon Tabasco sauce
1/4 teaspoon fresh-ground
  black pepper
1 teaspoon salt

1. On a baking sheet, spread the nuts in one layer.

2. In a small saucepan, melt the butter, then stir in remaining ingredients. (Or, alternately, place the butter in a heatproof cup or bowl and melt in the oven, then stir in remaining ingredients.)

3. Pour the butter mixture over the nuts and toss to coat evenly. Place in a preheated 300° oven for about 20 minutes, stirring several times. When done, nuts should be browned.

4. Pour the nuts into a bowl lined with paper toweling and let cool. If preparing ahead, store in a tin or covered jar. *Makes about 3-1/2 cups.* Can be stored for several months. If nuts become soggy, they can be recrisped in the oven before serving.

DATES (OR PRUNES) WITH BACON

I thought this was a concoction invented by a women's magazine food editor of yore until I was served them several times as a tapa in Spain. There, however, the dates were never pitted.

9 slices bacon   *18 pitted dates or prunes*

1. Cut the bacon slices in half and arrange on a baking sheet. Bake in a preheated 350° oven until half-cooked and still pliable. Drain the bacon on absorbent paper and wipe the baking sheet clean.

2. Wrap a half-slice of bacon around each date or prune and secure with a toothpick. Arrange on baking sheet. Bake in a preheated 350° oven, turning the rolls once, until bacon is crisp, about 3 minutes. *Makes 4 to 6 servings.*

FRIED CHEESE RAVIOLI

Frozen ravioli of at least acceptable quality can be found in almost every supermarket today and they make interesting appetizers when fried until crisp and golden, then sprinkled with plain or seasoned salt or served with a dipping sauce (see page 199).

1. Defrost them on paper toweling placed on a baking sheet.

2. In a large skillet, fry them in about 1/2-inch vegetable oil without crowding them. Be careful, because if the cheese leaks, they spatter.

3. Drain them well on absorbent paper, or, more efficiently, on a napkin-lined serving plate. They will be too hot to eat immediately, so you may hold the first batch until a second batch is finished, as long as you serve the first-made first. For a more elaborate presenta-

tion, serve the ravioli with parsley sprigs fried in very hot oil (you will have to add more to the pan) until just crisp.

GORGONZOLA CROQUETTES

1 cup cold milk
1/2 cup flour
2 tablespoons cold butter
1 egg
2 ounces fresh-grated
  Parmesan cheese
1/2 pound Gorgonzola cheese,
  cut into 1-inch cubes

Salt to taste
1/8 teaspoon Tabasco
1 egg
Fine dry breadcrumbs
Vegetable oil for frying

1. In a small saucepan, with a whisk, gradually blend the flour into the milk. Place over medium heat and, stirring occasionally with the whisk, cook until mixture becomes lumpy.

2. Remove from heat and beat until smooth. Add the butter in several bits and beat until completely absorbed. Beat in the egg.

3. Return to medium heat and beat until the mixture thickens to the consistency of mashed potatoes. If mixture is too thick, add a little more milk. If too thin, add another egg.

4. Beat in the two cheeses, salt to taste, and the Tabasco. Cool, then refrigerate until well chilled.

5. Place the egg in a small bowl and beat well with a tablespoon of water. Spread breadcrumbs on a dinner plate.

6. Using a teaspoon measure, scoop out heaping teaspoons of chilled cheese mixture and roll them into balls. Dip each ball in egg, coating well, then roll in the breadcrumbs. Arrange on a baking sheet as they are done. (May be prepared ahead, covered with plastic and refrigerated until ready to fry.)

7. In a skillet, heat at least an inch of vegetable oil until a pinch of breadcrumbs browns quickly. Fry the croquettes, without crowding, until browned all over. As they are done, remove with a slotted spoon and drain on absorbent paper. *Makes about 3 dozen.*

HERRING IN MUSTARD-DILL SAUCE

This was supposedly the favorite appetizer of the last king of Saxony, Frederick Augustus. At least his personal chef claimed it was when he served it at his next job, at Lüchow's, the turn-of-the-century German restaurant on 14th Street in New York. Lüchow's is one of the last reminders of 14th Street's glorious heyday and although the kitchen has its ups and downs I always find the carved paneling, the stained glass, the string orchestra, and the idea that Diamond Jim Brady and Lillian Russell ate there totally beguiling. The marinated herring will have a better texture and take fewer days to mature if you start out with fresh fish as they do at Lüchow's. But since fresh herring is often difficult to find and, when it is, it's sometimes hard to get the fishman to fillet, I've also given directions for salt herring. These must be soaked before they are marinated, but there is no cooking involved here at all, just soaking and marinating.

10 fresh herring (about 6 to
    the pound), filleted, or 20
    salt herring fillets
1 cup Düsseldorf mustard
1 cup peanut oil
4 tablespoons white wine
    vinegar
2 tablespoons lemon juice
    (1 lemon)

1 cup fine-chopped fresh dill
1/2 tablespoon fresh-ground
    black pepper
1/2 tablespoon salt
1/2 tablespoon whole allspice
2 tablespoons sugar

1. If using salt herring, rinse the fillets under cold running water. Place them in any stainless steel, pottery, or glass vessel and cover with cold water. Place in refrigerator and let soak for 3 days, changing the water daily.

2. On the day the fillets have finished soaking, in a mixing bowl, combine the mustard and oil. Beat with a wire whisk or fork until mixture has the consistency of mayonnaise.

3. Add vinegar in a thin stream, beating constantly. Beat in remaining ingredients.

4. In a deep dish or bowl, arrange the soaked salt herring fillets or the fresh fillets in layers, pouring sauce between layers. Top with more sauce. Marinate 3 days before serving. Serve with thin slices of pumpernickel or dark Scandinavian flat bread. *Makes 15 to 20 appetizer servings.*

MACKEREL IN WHITE WINE

A classic on French cold tables, the white wine marinade nicely counterbalances the fattiness of the mackerel. Ask the fishman to fillet the fish for you.

3 medium onions, sliced thin
3 cups dry white wine
1 teaspoon salt
8 whole peppercorns
1/2 teaspoon dried thyme,
  crushed fine

2 whole large bay leaves
4 pounds mackerel, filleted
1 lemon, sliced very thin and
  pitted

1. In a glass, enameled, or stainless steel saucepan, combine the onions, white wine, salt, peppercorns, thyme, and bay leaves. Bring to a boil. Boil vigorously until liquid has reduced by about a third.

2. Meanwhile, arrange the mackerel fillets in a glass, enameled, or stainless steel baking dish or au gratin pan. Arrange the lemon slices attractively on top of the fish.

3. Without disturbing the lemon slices, strain the boiling wine mixture over the fish fillets, reserving the onion rings.

4. Allow to cool to room temperature, then cover with plastic and refrigerate for 24 hours before serving. Chill the onion rings separately and use as a garnish. As an appetizer, serve with thin slices of very dense pumpernickel or black bread, sweet (unsalted) butter, and red

radishes. As a main course, serve with a rice salad. *Makes 10 to 12 appetizer servings, 6 to 8 main course servings.*

BAKED KIBBEH

Generally served as a main course, these rich squares of meat and bulgur wheat filled with pine nuts are also nice to serve when you want something a little more substantial than dips, spreads, and tidbits.

1-1/4 cups fine bulgur wheat
1/2 pound (2 sticks) butter, clarified (see note)
1/2 cup pine nuts (pignoli)
1 medium onion, fine-chopped
1/2 pound lean lamb, ground once
1/2 teaspoon salt

1/4 teaspoon allspice
1 medium onion, fine-chopped
1-1/2 pounds lean lamb, ground twice
1 teaspoon salt
1/4 teaspoon allspice
1/2 cup cold water

1. Place bulgur in a strainer and rinse under cold water for about a minute. Place in a small bowl and set aside.

2. Pour about 1/4 cup of the clarified butter into a 12- by 8-inch Pyrex baking dish and place in refrigerator so butter will solidify.

3. In a skillet, heat another 1/4 cup of the clarified butter over medium heat and sauté the pine nuts until just golden. Add the onion and lamb and continue cooking until lamb has lost its raw color. Stir in the salt and allspice and set aside.

4. In a large mixing bowl, combine the other chopped onion, the finely ground lamb, remaining salt, allspice, the reserved bulgur, and the water. With your hands, knead this mixture very well until it is rather pasty.

5. Pat half of the raw meat mixture into the bottom of the baking dish with the butter. Spread the cooked meat mixture evenly over this, then pat on the remaining raw meat mixture. Smooth out the top.

6. With a knife, cut a diamond pattern into the meat, cutting down to the bottom of the baking dish. Each one of these diamonds will be

a serving, so they should be about 2-1/2 inches wide. Pour over the remaining clarified butter. (May be prepared ahead to this point. Refrigerate until ready to bake.)

7. Bake in a preheated 375° oven for 40 minutes. Let rest 10 minute minutes before serving. *Makes 8 to 10 servings.*

Note: To clarify butter, which means to separate the yellow butter fat from the white milk solids, melt the butter in a small pan over moderate heat or in a heat-proof measuring cup in a moderate oven. Let the butter cool a few minutes, then spoon off the white foam on top. Carefully pour the clear butter fat off the milk solids that have settled to the bottom of the pan and reserve the butter for cooking. Clarified butter does not burn as readily as whole butter.

AROMATIC GLAZED PORK

This is excellent, albeit not Chinese, for sandwiches on crusty garlic bread.

Water
3 pound boneless pork
  shoulder
1 cup soy sauce (preferably
  dark Chinese soy)
1 3-inch piece of ginger,
  sliced thin

1 clove garlic, chopped fine
2 whole star anise (16 cloves
  of star anise)
6 tablespoons sugar
1 tablespoon dry sherry

1. If the meat is a long, flat piece, roll it up with the fattier side inside and tie into a bundle.

2. Bring a pot of water large enough to hold the pork roast to a rolling boil. (To know how much water to boil, place the roast in the pot, add water, then remove the roast.) Add the pork and allow to come to the boil again. In a colander, drain the pork, then rinse briefly under cold running water.

3. Place the pork back in the pot and add the soy sauce, ginger, garlic, and star anise. Bring liquid to a simmer, cover and let simmer slowly, turning occasionally, until tender, about 1-1/2 hours.

4. Remove the cover, add the sugar and dry sherry. Raise heat and allow the liquid to boil vigorously about 12 minutes, continually basting the meat and turning the meat occasionally. (A bulb baster really helps here.) When done, the meat should have a deep brown glaze. The liquid will be quite syrupy and will have reduced to about a cup.

5. Strain the cooking liquid. Slice and serve meat hot with hot sauce lightly brushed on the slices. Or, serve meat at room temperature with cooled sauce for dipping. *Makes about 10 to 12 appetizer servings.* May be prepared several days ahead.

Desserts

Apartment ovens are often too inaccurate or undependable for delicate cakes. Finding counter space to roll out pastries or knead dough is absurd. And storing more than a few basic baking pans is simply a luxury you can't afford. Nevertheless there are a good many baked desserts that a small kitchen can handle. I've selected only two cake pans — a springform pan and a tube pan — and given several recipes using each. None of them is so delicate, not even a rich cheesecake, that oven temperatures must be accurate to a degree. (There is a two-in-one type of springform pan that comes with a tube-pan insert, which would seemingly be perfect for a small kitchen. But the tube-pan recipes here rise too high for this pan. They require a high-sided pan, the kind used for angel food cakes, or a bundt pan.)

There's also a recipe for fudge pie I couldn't resist including that requires a pie plate. Although I don't think making pastry in small quarters is practical, owning a pie plate is. The right one can have multiple uses. I use a fairly deep 9-inch earthenware pie plate from a Pennsylvania pottery that doubles as a baking dish and looks attractive on the table. The Bennington Pottery in Vermont also makes a pie dish that is nice as a serving and baking or au gratin dish. It is relatively inexpensive and it's a 10-inch plate with straight sides so it doesn't necessarily look like a pie plate.

Occasionally you may succumb to the lure of frozen pie shells. I have tried a few brands made with butter and without preservatives that are actually better than many people's homemade ones. If you do use one of these, make sure to slip it out of its aluminum plate and into one of your own and give it a hand-finished edge or crimping.

For cookies and shortcake a baking sheet is necessary, but this is

221

also a multiple-purpose utensil not only for baking. (I often use a baking sheet simply to stack food on so it can be carried into another room and be out of the way. It can also act as a movable surface for draining bacon or other foods on paper towels. A rectangular baking pan is also versatile and not just for baking desserts. Although the inexpensive ovenproof glass type is perfectly functional for the oven, it is a little short on looks and can't be used on top of the stove or under a broiler. A better selection would be an attractive enameled metal pan that can be used no matter how high the heat or under the broiler when you want to brown the top of something, in effect an au gratin dish.

Most of these recipes can be mixed in one bowl or in one saucepan with just a wooden spoon or wire whisk. But an inexpensive electric hand mixer makes the work much easier and is essential if you ever want to make whipped cream. There is at least one mixer model that comes in its own wall case with a compartment for the beaters, and it can be hung on a pegboard. More basic models can be hung with large hooks through their handles or stored in a drawer. I think an electric beater is a necessity for anyone who is serious about dessert.

Plain fresh fruit is always a good dessert, of course, and requires no space at all to prepare. I always keep Amaretti di Saronno handy. These small crisp bitter-almond macaroons are delicious with pears, apples, peaches, nectarines, pineapple, strawberries, or fresh figs. I also like to crumble them on ice cream, serve them with coffee, and crumble them on sliced fruit sprinkled with white wine and sugar, arranged in a pie dish and baked with dots of butter until brown. Amaretti can be purchased in tins or boxes in Italian stores and specialty food shops. If you have the room, buy a large tin. They're cheaper in quantity and keep practically indefinitely.

Cheese is often served as dessert too. In fact, it more properly belongs in the main part of the meal or at the end than at the beginning as an appetizer. A cheese tray served with or without fresh fruit is most interesting with two or three different cheeses, although one perfect and luxurious cheese for dessert is never anything to complain about. There are very high-fat French cheeses called double and triple creams that are made specifically for dessert. Explorateur is the most unctuous, almost like eating whipped butter, but bland and soon tiresome to some tastes. Caprice des Dieux is another pleasant one, with a stronger flavor, and it is sold in some supermarkets in small oval wooden boxes. An honest cheese merchant with a wide selection of imported cheese is invaluable, though. Serve cheese at room temperature with unsalted crackers or crusty bread.

Keeping ice cream frozen is impossible in some small refrigerator freezer compartments, but if yours can handle it, ice cream is always an easy solution to the dessert problem. Included are several sauces with which to dress it up. You might also use the chocolate crumb crust recipe for an ice cream pie, which can be garnished with chopped, slivered, or sliced nuts, grated chocolate, or crumbled cookies.

CHEESECAKE

This has to be the easiest and most foolproof cheesecake recipe in existence. No exaggeration. It is all mixed in one bowl.

4 8-ounce tubs whipped cream
   cheese
1 pint sour cream
1/4 pound (1 stick) butter
1-1/2 cups granulated sugar

2 tablespoons cornstarch
1 teaspoon vanilla
1 teaspoon lemon juice
5 eggs

1. Into a large mixing bowl, empty the tubs of cream cheese and the container of sour cream. Do not mix.

2. Place the butter and sugar in the bowl, then sift the cornstarch into the bowl and sprinkle on the vanilla and lemon juice. Allow all the ingredients to stand, unmixed, until they reach room temperature.

3. With an electric mixer, beat all the ingredients together until mixed well. There will still be some lumps.

4. Beat eggs into mixture one at a time, mixing well after each addition. After all eggs have been added, mixture should be perfectly smooth.

5. Pour batter into a buttered 10-inch springform pan. Place springform into a larger roasting pan and half fill the large pan with hot water.

6. Bake in a 375° oven for 1 hour. Remove from oven. Let cool in water bath for 20 minutes, then remove from bath and cool to room temperature in the springform. After cooling, refrigerate at least 3 hours before serving, but remove from refrigerator about 30 minutes before serving to take off the chill. May be garnished with fruit as desired. *Makes about 12 servings.*

Variations: You may alter the flavoring by using 1/4 teaspoon almond extract instead of vanilla or 3 tablespoons dark rum or flavored liqueur instead of the extract. The cake has no crust, but you may sprinkle the buttered springform pan with ground or finely chopped nuts or fine dry breadcrumbs or cake crumbs.

LINZERTORTE

This rich nut pastry, with latticework on top and a filling of raspberry jam, makes a beautiful presentation and is easier to construct than the impression it gives. The dough is patted into the pan and you'll need no more than a few inches of counter space to form the lattice ropes.

1-3/4 cup all-purpose flour
3/4 cup sugar
1 teaspoon unsweetened cocoa
1 teaspoon baking powder
1/2 teaspoon cinnamon
1/4 teaspoon ground cloves
1/2 cup (1 1/4-pound stick)
  butter

1 egg
1 cup ground, blanched almonds
2 tablespoons lemon juice
2 tablespoons kirschwasser
  (optional)
1 cup raspberry jam

1. Place the flour, sugar, cocoa, baking powder, cinnamon, and cloves into a strainer balanced over a large mixing bowl. Sift them together into the bowl.

2. Cut the butter into pieces directly into the bowl, then add the egg, almonds, lemon juice, and (optional) kirschwasser. With an electric mixer, beat on medium speed until well blended. Chill dough for 30 minutes.

3. Divide the chilled dough into 3 equal parts. Pat one third of the dough into the bottom of a 10-inch springform pan.

4. Spread the raspberry jam on the dough in the pan, leaving about a 3/4-inch edge of dough exposed.

5. Divide each of the remaining two pieces of dough into 5 equal parts, yielding 10 pieces of dough.

6. On a flat surface roll each of the 10 pieces into a rope, 2 pieces to fit down the center of the torte, 4 slightly shorter to be placed about an inch from the center, and 4 even shorter to be placed near the edges. The shorter ropes will, of course, be thicker than the longer ropes. That's fine.

7. Lay 5 pieces parallel to each other across the top of the torte so they reach from edge to edge.

8. Arrange the remaining 5 strips on a diagonal over the first 5 strips. They should form a diamond pattern.

9. Bake in a preheated 350° oven for 30 to 40 minutes or until pastry is lightly browned. Cool 5 minutes, then remove outer ring of the pan. Cool thoroughly before serving. Torte is even better if allowed to "age" for at least one day. May be kept wrapped in foil for up to one week without a significant loss in quality. *Makes at least 8 servings.*

EASY-MIX POUND CAKE

This is a solid, rich pound cake on which to build your dessert fantasies with minor effort. It makes many servings but stays fresh enough when wrapped well to be eaten without embellishment for about a week. When it becomes dry, top it with fruit macerated in a little liqueur and natural fruit syrup, toast it and spread it with butter, grate it into cake crumbs for lining cake pans (see cheesecake, page 223), or douse it with rum for the foundation of a refrigerator cake (see note).

2 cups self-rising cake flour or 1 tablespoon baking powder and 1/2 teaspoon salt placed in a measuring cup with enough plain cake flour to make 2 cups
1/2 pound butter, at room temperature and cut into tablespoon-sized pieces
4 eggs
1/2 cup milk
1-1/2 cups sugar
1 teaspoon vanilla

1. In a large mixing bowl, place all the ingredients. With an electric mixer, beat for 5 minutes or until smooth and a light lemon color.

2. Spoon batter into a buttered and floured 10-inch tube pan and place in a cold oven. Turn oven on to 350° and bake for exactly 1 hour. Cool cake for 20 minutes in the pan, then remove and let rest at least 4 hours before serving. *Makes about 20 servings.*

Note: To make a refrigerator cake using a pound cake, butter a loaf pan, or a rectangular or square cake pan. Arrange 1/2-inch-thick slices of cake on the bottom and sides. Douse well with a mixture of rum diluted with strong coffee or water or a liqueur diluted with water. Spread on this a layer of mousse (see page 236), then another layer of doused cake. Cover with waxed paper and refrigerate overnight. Unmold and, if desired, pour on melted semisweet chocolate to cover the entire cake.

JEWISH APPLE-NUT CAKE

Another easy cake baked in a tube pan, this is an excellent coffee cake for brunch.

3 cups all-purpose flour
2 cups sugar
1 cup vegetable oil
4 eggs
1/4 cup orange juice
1 tablespoon baking powder

2-1/2 teaspoons vanilla
1 teaspoon salt
1 cup broken or coarse-chopped
   walnuts or pecans

5 medium apples
2 teaspoons cinnamon
5 tablespoons sugar

1. In a large mixing bowl, combine all the flour, sugar, oil, eggs, orange juice, baking powder, vanilla, and salt. With an electric mixer, beat until smooth. Stir in nuts.

2. Peel and core the apples, then chunk them into 1/2-inch pieces, letting them fall directly into a bowl. Add cinnamon and sugar. Toss together, then stir into the batter.

3. Scrape the batter into a greased and floured 10-inch tube pan. Bake in a preheated 350° oven for 1-1/2 hours. Cool upright in pan. *Makes about 10 servings.*

CREAM CHEESE COFFEE CAKE

Baked in a tube pan, this is a moist cake that will remain fairly fresh for several days.

1/2 to 3/4 cup chopped pecans
   or walnuts
1/2 cup sugar
1-1/2 tablespoons unsweetened
   cocoa
1 tablespoon cinnamon
1 cup butter (2 1/4-pound sticks)
1 8-ounce package cream cheese

1-1/2 cups sugar
1-1/2 teaspoons vanilla
4 eggs
2-1/4 cups all-purpose flour
1-1/2 teaspoons baking powder
3/4 cup dried currants or raisins
   (optional)

1. Generously butter a 10-inch tube pan, then sprinkle with nuts so that they stick to the sides and bottom. Set aside.

2. In a small bowl or cup, combine the 1/2 cup sugar, cocoa and cinnamon. Mix well. Set aside.

3. In a large mixing bowl, with an electric hand mixer, cream together the butter, cream cheese, sugar, and vanilla until light and fluffy.

4. Add eggs one at a time, beating well after each addition. Gradually beat in flour and baking powder. Stir in optional currants or raisins. Batter will be very thick.

5. Spoon half the batter into the prepared pan, then sprinkle with half the cinnamon-cocoa mixture. Spoon on remaining batter, then sprinkle on the remaining cinnamon-cocoa mixture. Even out the top, inevitably mixing some of the cinnamon-cocoa mixture into it.

6. Bake in a preheated 325° oven for 65 to 75 minutes or until top springs back when touched lightly near the center. Cool upright in pan for about 15 minutes, then remove from pan to finish cooling. *Makes about 10 servings.*

PAT'S KENTUCKY GLAZED ORANGE CAKE

Pat Kessler is the pastry chef at Aqua Manor and one of the chief reasons why this Long Island restaurant is so popular. With its bourbon glaze, this cake remains moist for several days.

1 cup (2 1/4-pound sticks) butter	3/4 cup orange juice
2 cups sugar	Grated rind of 1 orange
5 eggs	4 tablespoons butter
3 cups all-purpose flour	2/3 cup sugar
3 teaspoons baking powder	1/2 cup bourbon whiskey
1/2 teaspoon salt	

1. In a large mixing bowl, cream together the butter and sugar until light and fluffy.

2. Add the eggs one at a time, beating well between additions.

3. Onto a piece of waxed paper or into another bowl, sift the flour, baking powder, and salt together. Add to creamed mixture alternately with orange juice. Add orange rind.

4. Pour into a buttered and floured 10-inch tube pan and bake in a preheated 350° oven. Allow to cool for 10 minutes before removing from pan.

5. While cake is baking, prepare syrup. In a small saucepan, combine

the butter, sugar and whiskey. Heat, stirring occasionally, until sugar is completely dissolved.

6. While cake is still hot, poke several holes in it with a skewer. Slowly, to let it seep in, pour glaze over cake.

OATMEAL LACE COOKIES

These are delicate, elegant cookies, perfect with ice cream or sherbet. They are greasy when just coming from the oven, however, so make sure they drain thoroughly on absorbent paper before you serve them.

1/2 cup melted butter	*3/4 cup quick-cooking oatmeal*
1/2 cup sugar	*5 tablespoons all-purpose flour*
2 tablespoons milk	*1 teaspoon vanilla*

1. In a mixing bowl, combine all the ingredients and mix well with a wooden spoon.

2. Drop one rounded spoonful of the mixture onto an ungreased baking sheet for a trial. Bake in a preheated 350° oven for 8 to 10 minutes or until cookie has browned without burning at the edge.

3. Cool for about 30 seconds, then remove and place on absorbent paper. If cookie has spread and baked crisp and lacy, continue with rest of batter. If batter spread too much, add another teaspoon of flour. If batter is too stiff (unlikely), add another teaspoon of milk. *Makes about 2 dozen cookies.*

FORGOTTEN MERINGUES

The best way I can think of to use a few leftover egg whites, these are elegant in their way and handy to have around. In dry weather, they'll keep well in a tightly closed tin.

2 egg whites
1/8 teaspoon salt
2/3 cup sugar

1 cup chopped pecans
1 cup semi-sweet chocolate bits

1. Preheat oven to 350° for at least 20 minutes.

2. In a prefectly clean and dry mixing bowl, beat egg whites and salt with an electric hand mixer until thick and foamy.

3. Gradually adding all the sugar, continue beating until stiff.

4. Carefully fold in the nuts and chocolate. Drop by heaping teaspoonfuls onto a greased and floured baking sheet.

5. Place in the oven and turn it off immediately. Leave in the oven overnight (at least 12 hours) without even opening the door. *Makes about 2 dozen.*

Variation: Instead of nuts and chocolate, a combination of chopped dried fruits such as dates, raisins, figs and prunes may be used.

OATMEAL CHOCOLATE CHIP COOKIES

Next to the famous recipe for Toll House cookies, still on the back of the Nestlé's morsels package, these were the most popular cookies in my neighborhood when I was young—an almost identical recipe was printed on the back of the Quaker oatmeal box beginning in 1956.

3/4 cup butter, at room temperature
1 cup brown sugar
1/2 cup white sugar
1 egg
1/4 cup water
1 teaspoon vanilla

1 cup all-purpose flour
1 teaspoon salt
1/2 teaspoon baking soda
3 cups quick or old-fashioned oats
1 6-ounce package semi-sweet chocolate bits

1. In a mixing bowl, with an electric hand mixer, beat together the butter, both sugars, egg, water, and vanilla.

2. Sift the flour, salt, and baking soda into the bowl, then mix well. Stir in the oats and chocolate bits.

3. Drop by teaspoonfuls onto a greased baking sheet, spacing the cookies about 2 inches apart. Bake in a preheated 350° oven for 12 to 15 minutes. *Makes about 5 dozen.* (If you do not want to bake all the dough, it may be wrapped tightly and stored for several days in the refrigerator.)

OLD-FASHIONED STRAWBERRY SHORTCAKE

When the shortcake is still warm from the oven, the strawberries are sweet, and you take care to beat the cream just long enough to make it thick but not stiff, this can be an exquisite dessert. The short-cake can be prepared as much as several days ahead, dropped onto a baking sheet, and refrigerated until ready to go in the oven. The straw-berries can be prepared several hours in advance, but whipping the cream and assembling the dessert must be done at the very last moment. Although the preparation doesn't, the assembling *does* require some space, since each serving should be made on an individual plate. But this is one of those occasions when it is worth balancing plates on every available space.

2 cups all-purpose flour	1 quart strawberries
1 tablespoon baking powder	3 to 4 tablespoons sugar
3 tablespoons sugar	Kirschwasser or framboise liqueur
1/2 teaspoon salt	to taste (optional)
6 tablespoons butter	
3/4 cup milk	1 pint heavy cream
2 egg yolks	1 tablespoon sugar
	1/2 teaspoon vanilla (optional)

Softened butter (optional)

1. To make shortcakes, into a mixing bowl sift together the flour, baking powder, sugar, and salt.

2. Add the butter and either cut in with two kitchen knives or rub the dry ingredients with the butter between the fingertips until the mixture looks like coarse meal.

3. Measure out the milk, then add the egg yolks to the measuring cup and beat well with a fork.

4. Add the liquid to the dry ingredients and, with the fork, mix gingerly until dough binds together.

5. Onto a greased baking sheet, drop the dough off a large spoon, dividing the dough into six irregular mounds. Space the shortcakes at least 2 inches apart.

6. Bake in a preheated 425° oven for about 15 minutes or until the biscuits are tinged with brown.

7. To prepare berries, wash, hull and either cut them in half or slice them. Toss with sugar and optional kirschwasser. Do not let stand more than several hours.

8. To whip cream: Pour the cream into a mixing bowl and, with an electric hand beater, whip on high speed. After a minute, add the tablespoon of sugar and the optional vanilla. Whip just until cream is thick but still loose enough to run slowly off a spoon.

9. To assemble: When biscuits are done, let them cool a minute, then split in half with a fork, as you would an English muffin. Butter the shortcakes lightly, if desired, Place the bottom of each biscuit on a serving plate, cover with berries and some of their juice, then the top halves of the biscuits. Spoon whipped cream over each shortcake and top with a few more berries. Serve immediately. *Serves 6.*

Zabaione

In Italy, zabaione is eaten more as a restorative than as a dessert. Several sources even indicate that it is particularly recommended for reenergizing the body after lovemaking. I know one Italian, in fact, who served zabaione to his love almost every morning they were together, as well as whenever she had a cold. All this considered, it is still an excellent dessert, especially when cloaking a heap of berries.

I am offering two versions of zabaione here. One method, using an electric mixer, makes the light and foamy type most often served in Italian restaurants in America. It must be prepared just before it is eaten, although this takes only a few minutes. The second method, using a wooden spoon, which I learned from Giuliano Bugialli, the Florentine food authority, produces a concentrated custard that is folded into whipped cream and served cold. It can be prepared a day or so ahead if necessary. In either case, you must have an electric mixer, but the custard itself is done in just one small saucepan.

FOAMY ZABAIONE

6 egg yolks   1/2 cup Marsala wine
6 tablespoons sugar

1. In a 2- to 3-quart saucepan (preferably the smaller), with an electric hand mixer, beat the egg yolks and sugar together until light and lemon colored. Beat in the wine.
2. Place the saucepan in a skillet and almost fill the skillet with water. Remove the saucepan, then bring the water in the skillet to a boil over high heat.
3. When the water begins to boil, adjust heat so it will simmer steadily, then return saucepan with egg and Marsala mixture. Cook the zabaione, beating constantly with the electric mixer, until thick enough to form peaks. Remove from heat immediately and serve immediately. *Makes 4 servings.*

CREMA ZABAIONE

3 egg yolks   2 cups heavy cream
3 tablespoons sugar   2 heaping tablespoons sugar
1/2 cup dry Marsala wine

1. In a small saucepan, with a wooden spoon, beat the egg yolks and sugar together until light colored. Gradually stir in the Marsala.

2. Place the saucepan in a skillet and almost fill the skillet with water. Remove the saucepan, then bring the water in the skillet to a boil over high heat.

3. When the water begins to boil, adjust heat so it will simmer steadily, then return saucepan with egg and Marsala mixture. Cook the zabaione, stirring constantly, until mixture thickens enough to coat the spoon. This will happen just before the egg mixture is going to boil. Under no circumstances should you allow it to boil. Immediately remove from heat and continue beating for another 2 to 3 minutes. Set aside to cool, at least 1 hour.

4. In a mixing bowl, whip the cream with the sugar until it holds peaks. Carefully fold in the zabaione and serve. May be kept in a covered bowl in the refrigerator for several hours. *Makes at least 6 servings as an accompaniment to fruit, 4 served by itself.*

CREAMY RICE PUDDING

This is the style of rice pudding sold at many New-York-area diners and German delicatessens, only it tastes much, much better. I'm told New Englanders prepare it this way, too. I recommend it for a quick breakfast as well as a homey dessert.

3 cups whole milk
3/4 cup long-grain rice (not processed)
3 cups half-and-half (half cream, half milk)
3 eggs

3/4 cup sugar
1 teaspoon vanilla
1/2 cup raisins or currants (optional)
Cinnamon or nutmeg

1. In a 3-quart saucepan, bring the milk to a simmer. Gradually add the rice so the milk doesn't stop simmering. Stir, cover, and simmer

slowly for about 30 minutes or until the rice is tender and all the milk has been absorbed. Remove from heat.

2. Stir in the half-and-half and sugar.

3. In a small bowl, beat the eggs until well blended, then stir into the rice mixture.

4. Return mixture to medium heat and, stirring constantly, cook until mixture thickens enough to coat a wooden spoon.

5. Stir in the vanilla and the optional raisins or currants. Pour into a serving dish and sprinkle with cinnamon or nutmeg to taste. Chill well before serving. *Makes 6 servings.*

FRUIT FOOLS

A fool is nothing more than a fruit puree, or even just mashed fruits, folded into whipped cream. Fresh berries make the best fools, but when they aren't in season, unsweetend frozen berries are good, too. Many fool recipes tell you to cook the fruit in a sugar syrup, but I think the fruit flavors shine more when uncooked. The puree may be prepared ahead, but should be folded into the cream only at the last moment.

1 pint strawberries, washed and hulled, or 1 pint raspberries, blackberries, or blueberries, washed

Sugar to taste
2 cups heavy cream

1. In a mixing bowl, mash the berries with sugar to taste. Or, in a blender or food processor, puree the berries with sugar to taste. (If using seedy raspberries or blackberries, you will probably want to push the puree through a strainer to remove the seeds.)

2. In another bowl, whip the cream until it holds stiff peaks.

3. Fold the fruit puree into the whipped cream, then spoon into parfait or stemmed glasses. Serve very soon.

MOCK MOCHA MOUSSE

Called "mock" because if you are expecting a classic airy mousse you'll be disappointed. The classic mousse requires too much space to put together. This recipe is not quite mousse but quite delicious and very easy to execute.

8 ounces semi-sweet chocolate (preferably squares, not bits) 5 tablespoons brewed strong coffee	5 eggs, separated 2 tablespoons rum

1. In a heavy saucepan, combine the chocolate and coffee. Place over very low heat and allow chocolate to melt without stirring.

2. When chocolate has melted, remove from heat and mix together with the coffee. With a wooden spoon, beat in the egg yolks and rum. Set aside.

3. In a mixing bowl, beat the egg whites until stiff. Carefully pour the chocolate mixture down the side of the bowl with the egg whites, then gently fold together.

4. Pour into 4 serving cups or stemmed glasses. Refrigerate for at least three hours before serving. If chilling much longer, however, remove from refrigerator 20 to 30 minutes before serving. May be topped with whipped cream. *Makes 4 generous servings.*

Variations: To make a more mocha-flavored mousse, use a very strong brew of espresso instead of regular coffee. For an interesting contrast in flavors, fold 1/2 cup salted peanuts into the mousse, adding them with the chocolate mixture.

CHOCOLATE BROWNIES

Everyone loves good brownies, and I think this recipe is among the best. They also have the advantage of being prepared in one bowl. If you use cocoa instead of chocolate you don't even have to dirty a pot, out the brownies won't be as richly flavored.

2 cups sugar
3/4 cup butter
4 eggs
1 cup flour
1 cup cocoa or 4 ounces un-
    sweetened chocolate, melted

3/4 cup coarsely chopped walnuts
    or pecans
1 teaspoon vanilla
1 teaspoon brandy
Pinch salt

1. In a large mixing bowl, cream together the sugar and butter. Add the remaining ingredients and, with an electric mixer, beat on medium speed until will blended.

2. Spread in a buttered 11-1/4- by 7-1/2- by 1-1/2-inch Pyrex baking pan and place in a preheated 350° oven. Bake for 35 minutes, then cool in pan before serving.

CHINESE ALMOND FLOAT

A light, simple, but attractive dessert to end any dinner. If fresh berries aren't available, unsweetened frozen berries will do.

2 envelopes unflavored gelatin
2/3 cup cold water
1-1/2 cups boiling water
2/3 cup sugar
2 cups milk

1-1/2 teaspoons almond extract
1 quart strawberries or raspberries
1/3 to 1/2 cup sugar
Mint sprigs for garnish (optional)

1. In a large mixing bowl, slowly sprinkle the gelatin over the cold water. Let stand until gelatin has softened, about 5 minutes.

2. Add the boiling water and sugar. Stir until sugar and gelatin are completely dissolved.

3. Stir in the milk and the almond extract. Pour into a very lightly oiled 8-inch-square baking pan or other shallow pan. Chill until set.

4. At least 30 minutes before serving, in a serving bowl (clear glass

looks great), toss the berries with the sugar and let stand to form a syrup.

5. Just before serving, cut the almond gelatin into 1/2-inch squares and toss with the berries and syrup. *Makes about 8 servings.*

BAKED STUFFED PEACHES

When peaches are at their peak, this is a good fancy dessert. It is formulated for gingersnaps, but if you can get Amaretti, use them instead. If you want to get really extravagant, sauce these with crema zabaione.

*4 large, firm but ripe freestone
  peaches
1/4 cup sugar
Grated rind of 1 lemon
2 tablespoons unsweetened cocoa
1/4 cup blanched almonds,
  chopped fine (not ground)*

*5 gingersnaps, ground fine
1 tablespoon brandy
1 egg
2 tablespoons butter
1/4 cup sugar*

1. Bring a saucepan of water to a boil and plunge the peaches in for 1 minute. Remove with a slotted spoon and, when cool enough to handle, peel.

2. Cut the peaches in half and remove pits. With a teaspoon, scrape a little of the pulp out of each pit cavity and place the pulp in a small mixing bowl. Arrange the peach halves in a shallow baking dish as they are prepared.

3. To the peach pulp, add 1/4 cup sugar, the lemon rind, cocoa, almonds, gingersnaps, brandy, and egg. Mix well to form a thick paste.

4. Spoon the paste into the peach cavities, dot with butter, and sprinkle on the remaining sugar. Bake in a preheated 350° oven for about 25 minutes or until peaches are tender, but not collapsing. *Makes 4 servings.*

CARIBBEAN FUDGE PIE

It is definitely worth resorting to a good frozen pie shell in order to make this, but I've also included a recipe for a chocolate wafer crust if you want to go to the trouble of making this a double chocolate fantasy. The filling has the advantage of being entirely prepared in a small saucepan.

1/4 cup butter
12 ounces semi-sweet chocolate
1/4 cup rum
3/4 cup firmly packed brown
   sugar.
2 teaspoons instant coffee powder

3 eggs
1/4 cup all-purpose flour
1 cup coarse-chopped walnuts
1 unbaked 9-inch pie shell
1/2 cup walnut halves for top
   (optional)

1. In a small saucepan, combine the butter and chocolate. Over very low heat, let them melt together.

2. Stir in the rum, brown sugar, coffee powder, eggs, and flour, in that order. It should be a smooth mixture. Stir in the chopped walnuts.

3. Pour into the pie shell, then, if desired, decorate top with walnut halves.

4. Bake in preheated 375° oven for about 25 minutes or until filling is puffed and pastry edge is lightly browned. Cool thoroughly before serving. Serve at room temperature topped with whipped cream if desired.

CHOCOLATE WAFER CRUST

24 chocolate wafers
1/4 cup butter, at room
   temperature

1/4 teaspoon cinnamon

1. In a blender or food processor, pulverize the wafers into fine crumbs. (If you have the space, you can instead crush the wafers with a rolling pin between sheets of waxed paper.)

2. In a mixing bowl, mix together the crumbs, butter, and cinnamon.

3. Press mixture into an ungreased 9-inch pie plate. For a baked pie shell to be filled later, bake in a preheated 375° oven for 5 minutes.

CHOCOLATE MOUSSE PIE

Prepare the chocolate crumb crust and fill it with mock mocha mousse. Decorate with whipped cream and either chopped, sliced, or slivered nuts, grated chocolate or candied flowers and mint leaves.

RICOTTA, WHIPPED CREAM, POWDERED SUGAR, AND FRESH FRUIT

Next to fresh fruit, this is the easiest dessert I know. It is, nevertheless, very rich and almost a meal in itself. It is a dairy farmer's dessert but quite elegant-looking.

1 pound or a 15-ounch con-
    tainer ricotta cheese
1/2 cup heavy cream, whipped
    to soft, barely runny, peaks

Powdered sugar

1. Pile the cheese in a rough mound on a serving plate. (A white plate, if you want to continue the white-on-white motif.)

2. Heap on the whipped cream, letting it run down the sides of the cheese mountain, then sift sugar on top through a strainer.

3. Serve in a separate bowl, or surround the mound with, sweetened or unsweetened berries. Fresh whole peaches or peach slices or pineapple would be a good second choice. Or, you can serve it with separ-

ate bowls of chocolate chips or curls, unsalted nuts, or glacéed chestnuts purchased at a specialty food store. *Makes 2-3 servings.*

HONEY PRALINE SAUCE

Use on ice cream and dessert crepes.

1 cup firmly packed dark brown
  sugar
1/4 cup honey
Pinch salt
2 tablespoons butter

1/2 cup heavy cream
1/2 teaspoon vanilla
1 cup toasted pecan halves or
  pieces (see note)

1. In a saucepan, combine the brown sugar, corn syrup, salt, butter, and cream. Over medium heat, bring to a simmer, stirring constantly.

2. Simmer about 5 minutes, stirring occasionally, until mixture is thick and smooth.

3. Stir in vanilla and pecans. Cool at least slightly before using. If stored in the refrigerator, it will have to be heated to bring back to a syrupy consistency. *Makes about 2 cups.*

Note: To toast pecans, lay them on a baking sheet and place in a preheated 350° oven for 12 to 15 minutes, tossing once or twice so they will toast evenly.

HOT FUDGE SAUCE

If you keep a can of evaporated milk and a box of baking chocolate around, this will soothe you in the worst of emergencies. Remember, you don't have to wait for it to cool.

This recipe must originally have come from the back of an evaporated milk can, but it is smoother and, with a dash of cinnamon and nutmeg, more interesting than any commercial hot fudge I've eaten.

If you don't have ice cream or pound cake to put it on, dip fresh fruit into it.

1 large can (1-2/3 cups)
   evaporated milk
2 cups sugar
3 ounces (squares) unsweetened
   chocolate

1 teaspoon vanilla
1/4 teaspoon cinnamon
1/8 teaspoon nutmeg

1. In a small saucepan, combine the evaporated milk, sugar, and chocolate. Bring to a boil over medium heat.

2. With a wooden spoon, stir vigorously and continue boiling for 7 minutes or until dark and slightly thick. Remove from heat.

3. Add the vanilla, cinnamon, and nutmeg and beat with a wire whisk, rotary beater, or electric hand mixer for 1 minute. *Makes about 3 cupfuls.*

STRAWBERRIES IN TWO LIQUEURS

I've yet to find an explanation for it, but somehow the two unrelated liqueurs, crème de cacao and orange, make the strawberry flavor more pronounced. Barbara Rader of *Newsday* invented the combination by accident. Eat these as is, or use them as a sauce for ice cream or crepes (see cream cheese and nut filled crepes, page 244).

1 pint strawberries, hulled and
   washed
3 tablespoons sugar

2 tablespoon crème de cacao
2 tablespoons orange liqueur

Between 2 and 3 hours before serving, in a mixing bowl, toss all the ingredients together. Let stand at room temperature and do not chill. *Makes 2 to 3 servings.*

MELON BALLS WITH RUM AND BROWN SUGAR

A light but potent dessert.

1 medium melon of any kind   2 to 3 tablespoons brown sugar
1/2 cup light rum

1. Seed the melon and scoop the flesh out with a melon baller. Or, cut the flesh of the rind and cube it instead. Place the melon in a serving bowl.

2. Toss melon with rum and sugar and let stand a few minutes before serving. *Makes 2 to 3 servings.*

DESSERT CREPES AND FILLINGS

Crepes have become overwhelmingly popular in the last few years and, undoubtedly, they are both versatile and delicious. They are an easy thing to overdo, however. I also resent the hype they are getting from manufacturers of all sorts of new-fangled crepe pans, frozen crepe batter, and frozen baked crepes, and the impression given that they are something "gourmet" and difficult. In truth, the only equipment one needs for perfect crepes is a heavy and smooth-surfaced 6- or 7-inch skillet. And crepes are really no more difficult to prepare from scratch than pancakes, which is really all they are.

2 cups all-purpose flour   1/4 teaspoon salt
1 cup milk   2 tablespoons sugar
1 cup water   2 to 3 tablespoons brandy or
3 eggs   liqueur
1/4 cup melted butter

1. Place the flour in a mixing bowl. Pour in the milk and water. With a whisk or electric mixer, beat to mix. Add the eggs and beat until

smooth. Stir in the melted butter, salt, and sugar. Let stand at least two hours before using. (If there are any lumps in the batter, just strain it.)

Alternately, combine all the ingredients, except brandy or liqueur, in a blender or food processor and process a few seconds until smooth.

2. Heat a 6- to 7-inch skillet over medium-high heat until very hot. Meanwhile, stir the brandy or liqueur into batter.

3. Test one crepe before proceeding with all the batter: Grease the skillet very lightly, then, holding skillet in right hand (left, if you are left-handed), pour about one-quarter cup batter into the center of the skillet. Rotate the skillet so batter will cover evenly. Pour any excess batter back into bowl. Return to heat and cook until bottom has browned lightly and edges begin to brown, about 90 seconds. Lift edge of crepe with a fork or spatula. Turn with fingers and bake on other side about 30 seconds. Turn out onto a kitchen towel and if crepe is satisfactory, continue with remaining batter. (It is not usually necessary to grease the pan after the first crepe.)

4. If batter is too thick, add water by the tablespoon until desired consistency is reached. If too thin, beat in flour a teaspoon at a time until desired consistency is reached. *Makes 12 to 16 crepes.*

CREAM CHEESE AND NUT FILLED CREPES

These can be baked, filled, and arranged on a serving platter well in advance and can be served with either hot fudge (page 241), praline sauce (page 241), or, best, with strawberries in two liqueurs (page 242).

1 8-ounce package cream cheese
6 ounces pecans or walnuts,
*   ground fine*
2 tablespoons milk

2 tablespoons confectioners' sugar
12 dessert crepes
sauce of choice

1. In a mixing bowl, cream together the cream cheese, walnuts, milk, and sugar until smooth and spreadable.

2. With a kitchen knife, spread a thin layer of the cheese mixture on each crepe. Roll loosely and arrange the crepes on a serving platter. Cover with plastic and refrigerate until ready to serve.

3. Remove crepes from refrigerator about 30 minutes before serving. Immediately before serving, pour on sauce of choice. *Makes 6 servings.*

CREPES WITH WALNUT BUTTER AND CHOCOLATE

These are simple and quick, but both the crepes and the plate they are served on must be hot. Wrap pre-prepared crepes in two aluminum foil packages of 3 crepes each. Heat in a 350° oven for 20 minutes, or 25 or 30 minutes if the crepes are frozen. Place a heatproof serving dish in the oven for the last few minutes.

1/2 cup (1 1/4-pound stick) butter, at room temperature
1/4 cup confectioners' sugar

8 ounces walnuts, ground fine
6 hot crepes
2 ounces bittersweet chocolate

1. In a mixing bowl, cream together the butter and sugar. (May be done in advance.)

2. Spread each hot crepe with a heaping tablespoon of butter, sprinkle generously with walnuts, roll or fold in quarters, and place on the hot serving dish.

3. When all crepes are arranged, grate chocolate over them with a rotary hand grater. *Makes 2 or 3 servings.*

Index